IN GRANDPA'S FOOTSTEPS

For Helen
In fond remembrance
Douglas

IN GRANDPA'S FOOTSTEPS

A 92-year-old shows how to start a new career at 60

Douglas Dickins, FRPS

The Book Guild Ltd
Sussex, England

The Book Guild Ltd.
25 High Street
Lewes, Sussex

First published 2000
© Douglas Dickins

Set in Bembo
Typesetting by
Acorn Bookwork, Salisbury, Wiltshire

Printed in Great Britain by
Thanet Press Ltd, Margate, Kent

A catalogue record for this book is
available from the British Library

ISBN 1 85776 459 5

Contents

Reel 5 Action Moves West

Reel 6 The Drop of the Curtain

For Eibhlin

The life that I have
Is all that I have
And the life that I have
Is yours.

The love that I have
Of the life that I have
Is yours and yours and yours.

A sleep I shall have
A rest I shall have
Yet death will be but a pause.

For the peace of my year's
In the long green grass
Will be yours and yours and yours.

Code poem by Leo Marks for use by SOE agents

Acknowledgments

As a computer-illiterate, I owe thanks to Mark Hughes, my publisher grandson-in-law, for opening my eyes to the mystery of book production on a machine which his primary-school children can operate, and for useful advice on publishing in general.

I thank also Karina Zabihi, an Anglo-Persian lady who edited my draft in the early stages and criticised pungently, notably on the Persian and Russian chapters.

I am most grateful to Sir Hugh Cortazzi, GCMG, our former Ambassador at Tokyo in 1980–84, for writing a Foreword, and for the loan of a woodcut print by Hirosige III, the nineteenth-century artist who was contemporary with my Grandpa.

It would be ungenerous not to record the part played by my wife Eibhlin in our travels. Not only did she accompany me on lengthy tours on India, Malaysia, Singapore, South Africa, Morocco, Egypt, Greece, Turkey, Hong Kong, the Caribbean, and many times in Canada and the USA, but she performed the vital role of passenger, so important when taking a right-hand drive car on the continent. Without the extra pair of eyes, every passing manoeuvre would be a hazard, and her calming presence acted as a brake on my road rage.

For her sister Breda and her husband Gordon who lacked a car until the 1970s, we often provided transport for a foursome. We had an electric kettle plugged into the car battery, enabling the invigorating 'cuppa' to be ready without delay on comfort stops. Picnics were an economy besides being fun. Gordon, the son of a vicar, was besotted with architecture, and as route-finder would cunningly include detours to baroque or gothic in the Tyrol. If he was dubbed the 'church-hound', I qualified as the 'pass-hound', being never happier than pitting myself against the steepest gradients and tightest hairpin bends of Europe's highest mountain passes. The Gross Glockner in Austria's Hoher Tauern reaches 8212 ft, and the Stelvio, Europe's highest border between Switzerland and Italy at 9045 ft with 49 hairpins is usually open only between June and October. Once, when crossing the latter in June, with the road excavated from 10 ft snowfields, there was a slight avalanche in front of us, then another behind us, causing a delay of an hour or two before the ever-alert road workers came up to clear the route.

Happy days! – which illuminate my memories.

Foreword

By Sir Hugh Cortazzi, GCMG, HM Ambassador at Tokyo 1980–1984

It is never easy to write a readable memoir at any age. To write one at the age of 92 is an achievement which many much younger people must envy. Douglas Dickins has not only done this but has produced a book which is vivid, colourful and amusing.

Douglas Dickins' book spans three generations from his grandfather's life in Japan nearly a century and a half ago, through his father's service in India to his own life in the twentieth century. He began his travels early on, visiting the Caucasus in Stalinist times. While serving in the RAF in the Second World War he returned to India where he had lived in childhood. But his life as a professional travel writer did not really begin until he was able to retire from the humdrum life of a bank.

Douglas Dickins, as he tells his readers, always had a strong interest in photography. He learnt this trade, or perhaps we should say this art, the hard way before modern cameras with electronic eyes and other devices has been invented and before developing and printing had become mechanised. At one time he thought of becoming a portrait photographer, but perhaps fortunately he refrained from pursuing this aspect of photography and devoted his talents to the portrayal of people and scenes which he encountered in his wide ranging, interesting and often exciting travels round the world.

F. V. Dickins, Douglas's grandfather, was a colourful character and scholar who first went to Japan as a naval surgeon and returned there as a barrister. He was a friend of the formidable Sir Harry Parkes, who was head of the British mission in Japan from 1865 to 1882 and wrote the Japan part of the two volume life of his friend. Douglas's father visited Japan while serving in the East. Following in his footsteps Douglas found much to interest him in modern Japan.

Douglas Dickins' book is copiously illustrated wth a selection from his massive library of photographs. These show his great talent as a photographer and his understanding of people and scenes.

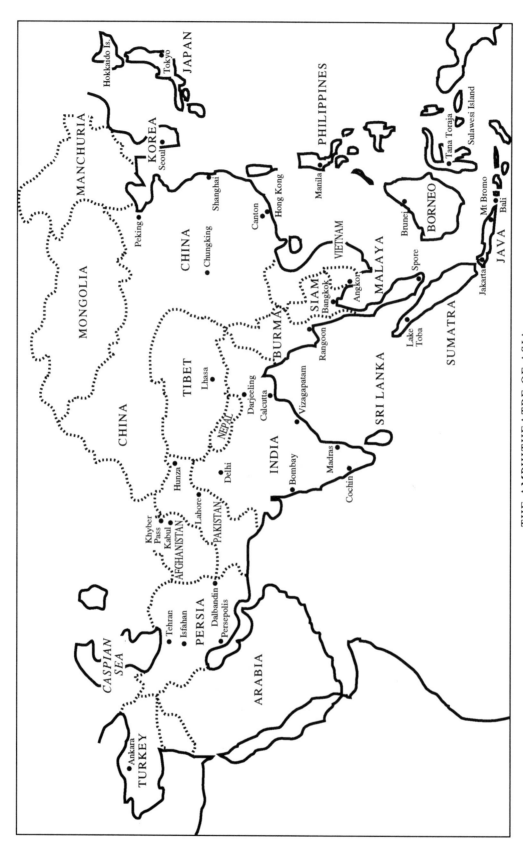

THE AMPHITHEATRE OF ASIA

REEL 1

Youth and Service

1

Introduction

Conceived in Rangoon, born in a Wiltshire manor house and shipped at 6 months by P&O to Calcutta: what else could I become but a traveller? So I was; but not until my sixtieth birthday could it be done 'my way'.

What took you so long, you may well ask? Too late now to say *mea culpa*. Was it the throw of the dice, or lethargy, or patience that made me stick it out in a routine office job to pensionable age? When does choice take over from fate? In truth, an early marriage gave few chances of long-haul travel before finishing the stint of 42 years of pen-pushing. So I think it was mainly patience.

In these moving pictures which are life, and in which we are all extras but few get speaking parts, my plot was simple. I just wanted to travel wherever I chose, to explore and understand the diversity of the world; and to pay my way as far as possible by writing and photography. Sorry it took so long to get started, but for the last 32 years it has been working out as planned.

It was inevitable that Asia should figure topmost in my imagination, for my father, Frederick, was a Brigadier in the Indian Army, where my childhood was spent; and his father, Frederick Victor Dickins had known Japan first from 1864 to 1866 as a surgeon in the Royal Navy, and later as a barrister living in the concession of Yokohama from 1871 to 1879. He there raised two aunts and an uncle. My father was born at home in 1879. A grandmother was born in Madras. So Asia was in the blood.

During the 42-year slog much of my travel had to be vicarious. There was always travel in books. First, Kipling's *Jungle Book* kept India alive for me, and childhood imagination roamed a world where cowboys and Indians were always massacring each other and the buffaloes. Intrepid explorers were risking cannibals to 'discover' unknown lands where in fact the native inhabitants had been living for centuries. Slave traders were pursued by the Royal Navy. Pirates ranged the oceans and buried their loot on desert islands. Criminals were brought to justice by Sherlock Holmes. Missionaries risked their health and their lives to bring the truth as they saw it to the heathen.

Later in adult life, Peter Fleming brought us *News from Tartary*, and had a *Brazilian Adventure* with piranhas. Alexandra David-Neel made us almost believe in the *Mystics and Magicians of Tibet*. Heinrich Harrer spent *Seven Years in Tibet*, and tutored the Dalai Lama. Wilfred Thesiger braved the perils of castration in the *Danakil Diary of Abyssinia*, where dried testicles are a warrior's trophy, the bar mitzvah of a savage race. Arthur Grimble traced the *Pattern of Islands* in the Pacific, and on radio too.

Reading is no substitute for travel, but it surely helps to assuage the pangs of wanderlust; and is both a preparation for future travel and an education in living which continues throughout life for the young in heart.

Life was never dull. With petrol at 1s. 2d. (6p) a gallon, I ran a motor bike from age 16, then a sporty Morgan three-wheeler with overhead valve Anzani engine; which was fine until one of the wheels dropped off on a corner in Streatham. It was ten years before I bought my first car, a 14hp open French Ballot, for £9. It had so many faults (leaky radiator, defective starter often needing a push start) that I sold it three months later – for £19.

In 1930 I entered the Scottish Six Days Trials with my 500cc Norton, in a triple capacity, as competitor, reporter and photographer. The result was published in *Motor Sport* in three pages, for which I received the princely sum of six guineas – about a week's wages. After nine years, my salary was £280 *per annum* – in real money, for we were on the Gold Standard between 1925 and 1931.

So in my twenties I was already a journalist, while being a banker from nine to five – or very much later – moonlighting if you like, though there was no law against pursuing journalism and photography as relief from the routine job. I even toyed in the 1960s with the idea of becoming a portrait photographer, and offered a service of 'home portraiture' which earned a few pennies, largely owing to the proximity of the Monkey Club, that exclusive ladies' finishing school whose nubile products provided ideal models. This was very exhausting at the end of a hard day's work, for I did my own processing including early varieties of colour printing by the Agfa system which required five separate chemical baths, taking one hour to produce a single print or a test strip. As a competition-wallah, a few 20 × 16 inch prints won acceptance in international exhibitions.

I also took a full technical course of photography under Professor Margaret Harker at the Regent Street Polytechnic. Through the medium of local photographic societies where we all competed in exhibiting and criticising each other's work, I 'graduated' into becoming a club lecturer and judge, travelling to provincial clubs or societies as 'guest lecturer'. All in the good cause of appreciating the art of photography; for all photographers are amateurs at heart, are they not? And in black and white, when there were 'rules' of composition to be learnt, and skills of manually controlling tone to be mastered. Looking back, I wonder how I ever had the nerve to criticise anyone else's work – for 'art' is all so subjective, is it not?

Today there are no rules. A dead sheep or a pile of bricks is 'art'. Or is it?

Long before our sixties, holiday travel with my wife had searched the byways of England and Scotland, of Europe from Cape St Vincent to the Dardanelles, and probed into North Africa. The car was the liberator and aeronautics helped to make a holiday go further by aerial car freighters which humped their heavy loads over the Channel from Lydd to Ostend, or even further to Basle. I published and illustrated the story of our travels in motoring magazines and others such as *Country Life*, *The Lady*, *Field*, *Homes & Gardens* and the *Daily Telegraph*. I was also building up a photo library for the use of travel brochures. Today book illustrations are more important and the library is a well-known specialist on Asia.

A guardian angel oversaw fate sometimes. As an RAF officer I was posted to Singapore in February 1942, but the Japanese got there first. Bonus number one. So it was India instead. Bonus number two, for my Edwardian–Indian childhood made it seem like home. On 'retiring' at 60, it was the most natural thing in the world to take the overland route to India by coach – the journey that changed my life. This was only made possible by an understanding wife (bonus number three) who, after discussing our project for a do-it-yourself safari by Dormobile, decided to let me do it alone. As Kipling said, 'He travels the fastest who travels alone'.

Two months and 11,000 miles later, I arrived in New Delhi with a commission from the Indian Tourist Office for an introductory tour of three weeks, expanded at my own expense to two months. This was the first of seven tours over the next 20 yeras. My plot was thickening, and I was photographing with three cameras in colour and black and white. Today my photo library covers the five continents and almost all of Asia. It illustrates books on eastern religions, art and architecture. But there is so much more to see and learn: perhaps I must wait for the next life?

Life is full of ironies and it is a typical one that, having fought against the Japanese with fierce detestation of their atrocities, I should have found it easy, in four visits 30 years later, to understand my Grandpa's love of a country so beautiful, with a people so polite, orderly and conformist – though always unfathomable.

I could not have known, then, how closely my future travel plans would follow in the footsteps of both Grandpa and Father, leading even further afield to a wider world than they knew, and by means of transport that they never dreamed of.

This book is a memoir, not an autobiography, so I beg leave to hop about a bit; and if, like the frog who jumps ahead of himself (this suggest a Zen *koan*: *why* does a frog jump ahead of himself?), I sometimes land in a murky pool, then I suggest that the reader presses on into the next non-sequitur. For, like the Canadian Mountie whose training Depots I photographed in Ottawa and Regina in Saskatchewan, I generally get *somewhere* in the end.

2

Reality in Russia

He walked by himself, and all places were alike to him.
    'The Cat that Walked by Himself' Kipling, Just So Stories

If you live long enough, everything comes full circle. Skirts go up and down; men's ties wax fat and shrink to skeletal. Capitalism gives way to communism, which completes its circle by going bust.

In the 1930s the Soviet Union was hailed by Sidney and Beatrice Webb in their giant work of research as a 'New Civilisation'. As we now know, at the time Stalin was shooting his Generals, putting British businessmen on show trials as 'spies' and forcibly collectivising the *kulaks* or prosperous peasants. None of this was visible to a tourist, but the poverty was. People in the street wanted to buy the capitalist clothes off your back. These blemishes were overlooked by such pundits of the great and good as H.G. Wells, Professors J.B.S. Haldane and J.D. Bernal. Lenin had a word for these western experts who were dazzled by the surface appearance of communism. They were, he said, 'useful idiots'.

I may have been an idiot, though certainly not a useful one. The attraction for me was the remarkable cheapness of a Russian holiday; Intourist charging £1 a day, all-in ('hard class'). The idea of a holiday in the mountain country of Georgia, lying in the Caucasus whose peaks of 18,000ft were reminiscent of the Himalayas, was attractive. Having read a little history, I knew how the Tsar's troops had fought for nearly a century to overcome the stubborn resistance of tribes – parallelling Britain's attempts to subdue the unruly North-West Frontier of India.

Both Georgia and Armenia had been Christian since the fourth century, and they were annexed by Catherine the Great in the eighteenth. This left the Caucasian mountain mass riddled with petty principalities, much given to tribal feuding and fiercely opposed to Russian control. These patriarchal clans, especially in Azerbaijan and Daghestan, were Muslim, and they fought a *jihad* (holy war) which forced the Tsar, in the early 1800s, to build the Georgian Military Highway for transporting troops and artillery to subdue them; a success not finally achieved until the 1880s. The guerilla chieftains of this colonial struggle were romanticised by Tolstoy, Pushkin and Lermontov; but these literary giants also fought in the Tsar's army as good imperialists.

Every journey starts with a step, and in June 1938 my first step was as an independent traveller on a flight by a tri-motor Fokker from Croydon's grass airport, to Amsterdam to catch the Moscow night express – thereby saving an extra day of my 12 days' holiday.

A week in Moscow, with a pretty Intourist guide to show me the sights, including a cruise on the newly opened Moscow–Volga canal; two nights of opera at the Bolshoi, seeing Tchaikovsky's *Eugene Onegin* and Borodin's *Prince Igor*; and a visit to an open prison where young hoodlums were supposed to be cured by playing netball among birch trees in the Lenin Hills – who's kidding? – these were my introduction to Soviet culture.

Going south by train in 'hard class', the hardness of the solid wooden benches was scarcely mitigated by a thin mattress. Constant tea came from a samovar bubbling at the end of the corridor. Every stop brought *babushkas* in white headscarves to offer eggs and chickens to passengers. Meals and small talk with the aid of a dictionary were shared with the friendly but suspicious proletariat. We ran through endless wheatfields, birch forests, and for miles along the banks of the Don. Forty-four hours later we reached Ordzhoni-kidze, 1,800ft up in the foothills. Formerly called Vladikavkaz, meaning Conqueror of the Caucasus, it marked the start of the Georgian Military Highway.

The hundred miles to Tiflis (now Tbilisi) were covered daily by a public bus, a Soviet-built Ford, an open 'charabanc' carrying eight passengers on bench seats ranged crosswise. Apart from a couple of punctures and quenching a thirsty engine with water collected from the river in an old inner tube, the journey, including a climb to 8,000ft went without incident.

As we climbed the densely forested valley of the Terek, it became evident that the Caucasus are comparable to the Himalayas rather than the Alps. We bumped over loose boulders and crossed watersplashes where snow-fed tributaries had washed away the road. In the Daryal Gorge, where the road was cut out of vertical cliffs, it took the Tsar's engineers eight years to advance five miles, fighting much of the time. Occasional villages were guarded by forts. Above the treeline there were few signs of life but sheep and goats and herdsmen riding with their square-shouldered cloaks and fur hats. At the summit, snowdrifts lay by the road and wooden tunnels protected against avalanches. A stop at Kazbek village showed a handful of houses, a bridge washed away, and high above towered the snowclad peak of Mount Kazbek at 16,512ft.

On the Georgian side, the road descended with many hairpin bends, clinging to dizzy-making slopes, overlooking rooftops of stone huts, rivers far below, and an ocean of snow-tipped mountains. Gentians, crocus and wild tulips flowered among scanty crops, and pigs rooted in a deserted graveyard.

At Passanaourskaya we eight passengers lunched on shashlik, onions and flat unleavened bread, in an open restaurant covered in creepers. A jovial Red Army officer pressed me to share his cherries and Georgian wine. An old beggar crossed himself and blessed me for a very small tip – something that is not supposed to happen in the Soviet Union.

Georgia had been conquered by the Red Army only 17 years before, and was plainly an Asiatic colonial country. Even today Russians form only 7.4 per cent of its population; Armenians 9 per cent, and Azeris (Asiatics from Azerbaijan) another 5 per cent.

Arrival in Tbilisi coincided with an election, which had brought into the city many examples of the minorities: Cossacks, Kurds, Tartars, Turkmen, Persians, Armenians, Jews, Ossetians, Chechens, Daghestanis, Kazakhs, Uzbeks. Many were Asiatics with flowing robes and turbans, but there were no mosques or other evidence of their religion. A few Christian churches were open, but Stalin had been hard on Islam, rightly judging it as incompatible with communism. Over 1 million Muslims had fled to Persia and Turkey. At least there are no more tribal feuds, Stalin said, though Muslims worship at their peril. How predictably that has come full-circle! And how prophetically it warns of the folly of supposing that the disparate and differently-motivated peoples of Europe can be forced into a common mould and required to call themselves 'Europeans'.

Tbilisi, a city of 1 million, is dominated by a seventh-century Persian fort, high above the river Tura. Narrow cobbled streets and crumbling houses of the upper city contrasted with broad tree-lined avenues and the university of the modern city. Shops were open until midnight, selling hunting and fishing equipment, silver filigree and jewellery, glass, china, and handicrafts such as tailoring and shoemaking. Jamaica rum, French brandy, Grande Chartreuse and Benedictine, all Soviet imitations, were on sale, and in the cafés were strawberries and rich cream cakes. Prices were high, but there seemed to be no shortages of food. Georgia is a rich country, producing 95 per cent of Russia's tea, and the bulk of her wine and fruit.

The election was celebrated with a parade of soldiers, cavalry, militiamen in white uniforms, men and women in national costume, marching through the main square and Rustaveli Propect, ending in the Park of Culture with searchlights and fireworks. Here crowds sat under the trees among fountains and ice-cream stands, while loudspeakers blared out music. At the next table, four Georgians sat down to dine at 11 p.m. and ordered eight bottles of wine, from which they toasted each other ad lib. The parachute tower was being used by scores of children under moonlight. It looked pretty, but, 'once bitten, twice shy'. My ankle was still sore from the encounter in Moscow.

My diary is silent on the return journey by the same bus and driver, for I suffered from the Curse of the Caucasus, and arrived in Ordzhonikidze much the worse for wear, just in time to catch the night train to Rostov on Don and Kiev, stops on the way home.

How much wool was pulled over my eyes? Not a lot, for although I was taken to showpiece collective farms and fed dubious statistics, I also wandered freely on my own, photographing the slummy conditions in old Tiflis.

To the Russians' disillusionment with communism is added the volcanic eruption of Islam – the joker in the pack, not merely in Transcaucasia but in all the Asiatic republics further east, which constitute 40 per cent of the population. The Muslims are suffering double frustration; from Russian colonialism, and from religious resentment of the infidel government. How much they hated it was not evident when I was in Georgia. *Glasnost* has lifted the curtain, but it was a surprise even to Gorbachov when the time bomb of Azerbaijan blew up in his face.

A good understanding of the background is given by Amir Taheri's *'Crescent in a Red Sky'* a scholarly book, surveying the history of Soviet Muslims. Amir Taheri is an Iranian who understands the menace of Muslim fundamentalism, threatening to spread worldwide from the Ayatollahs of Iran – for me a plague more pestilent even than communism.

Sixty years have not dimmed my memories of the kindliness and friendliness of the Georgians; their lovely women and handsome, wideawake men, of whom it is said that if a Georgian enters a revolving door behind you, he may well come out in front.

3

Flying Dreams

Myself when young did eagerly frequent
Doctor and Saint, and heard great argument
About it and about, but evermore
Came out by the same door as in I went.

The Rubaiyat of Omar Khayyam, Stanza 27

Baulked of a lifelong desire to fly a plane, I was too old for flying training in the RAF in 1941, but as a 7-year-old in 1914 the memory survives of a biplane taking off from a field behind my Grandpa's house. A mysterious event, it may have been a cousin of my father's who was in the Royal Flying Corps, making an unauthorised visit from a training camp on nearby Salisbury Plain. It thrilled me and gave me the urge to fly, but it was not until the age of 85 that I attained the sensation if not the actuality of flying my own plane.

It was on a simulator at Gatwick. The controls of the DC10 and the sensation of movement were identical to the real thing. Take-off from Heathrow was 'a piece of cake' as we used to say in the war. 'Where would you like to land?' asked the Captain. From all the world's airports which can be displayed on the simulator, I chose Hong Kong's Kai Tak; both because it is difficult and because I know it well. It was a night approach. 'Just head for the chequer-board in the middle of Kowloon,' said the Captain, 'and when you cross over a line of red lights, turn right ninety degrees.' Sure enough, there among the housetops was the brightly-lit runway, a narrow concrete pier extending into the harbour. To control the angle of descent (the glide path), you watch four white and four red lights, either side of the runway. See two white and you are too high. See one red and one white, straighten up. See four reds and start praying – or abort the landing. We made it a couple of times, and aborted once. The really difficult part, I found, was after touchdown when you must forget about steering with your hands, and start steering the single front wheel with your feet, simultaneously controlling the brakes by pressing down hard on the pedals with your toes.

Repeating the exercise two years later on the latest 747-400 with modern fly-by-wire controls where instructions are dialled in by computer, I found the changing of altitude more difficult to read than the old rotating clock hands. We landed safely again, but on the last landing my feet were cack-handed and over-corrected the front wheel which wandered about like a supermarket trolley, while I pressed even harder on the brakes – so we drifted onto the grass verge, and maybe got a bit wet.

Although I did take a commercial flight before the last war, the first experience of flying 'in the trade' so to speak, was with Catalina and Sunderland flying boats in the RAF at Stranraer in Scotland. I straightway fell in love with the 85-knot Catalina and its big brother, the four-engined Sunderland. Though being trained as an Ops Room Controller, we were encouraged to get in as much flying time as possible, to make us sympathetic to the pilots' problems. This was an invitation to joyride. No take-off on land can equal the excitement on water, when the streamlined hull of a flying boat 'rides on the step', and with windscreen and side gunport blisters drenched with spray finally drags itself apart from the ocean which tries to stick to it, and soars aloft, 50 tons defying gravity. Then the ocean's surface must be read like a sailor to determine the wind's direction. There are no wind socks at sea. I was even permitted to take the controls and fly a Cat around Ailsa Craig, the island in the Firth of Clyde. No wonder I love Cats of both varieties.

The next meeting with a Cat was in the monsoon of 1942 when we were 'holding the fort' at Cochin on India's Malabar coast. The Eastern War was still at a critical stage: Singapore had fallen in February, and by midsummer Burma was occupied, Calcutta had been bombed, and fighter planes used the *Maidan* to take off in defence. This was far removed from our south-western coast, where our concern was the sea war, as part of 225 Group of Coastal Command – shunted here from our aborted posting to Singapore – never more welcome!

Japan's navy was in control of the Indian Ocean, where 100 ships had been sunk in the month of April alone, and the only modern RAF aircraft in the region – in nearby Ceylon – had been decimated by aerial attacks. India's coasts were wide open to invasion, and our few hundreds of newly-arrived airmen were plugged into the Indian Air Force's newborn Coast Defence Flights. Ours was No. 5; others were set up at Calcutta, Karachi, Madras and Vizagapatam. All were created, shortly before the war started, by civilian pilots and businessmen, British and Indian, in the manner of our pre-war University Volunteer Reserve Squadrons.

Starting pretty much from scratch, we were struggling to put down a concrete runway on the civil airstrip, amid seas of mud and daily rain. The whole island on which airport and railway station are built had only been dredged from the shallow harbour ten years before. Commanded to create an operations room, I secured the wooden packing case in which a Fulmar aircraft had been delivered to the Fleet Air Arm (which also shared our runway) and cut out a door and windows to form my 'office'.

It was a welcome sight when a Catalina put down in Cochin's lagoon harbour in August 1942. Our first problem was to clear a landing path among the ferries, fishing canoes, heavy wooden cargo wallums and commercial steamers that swarmed all over the harbour. With the aid of a megaphone and the Harbourmaster's launch we managed to convince the unbelieving that an aeroplane was actually going to land on water – something they had probably never seen before. Having finally got her down the next problem was landing the crew. The Harbourmaster's launch had a mast, so could not be got under the wing. The solution was to commandeer a fisherman's canoe and by this means they were ferried ashore, recorded by my camera. Alas, we were not to derive any benefit from this Cat, with its wonderful capacity for staying aloft for up to 27 hours, for the visit was only brief and it returned to base in Ceylon.

Among the wide variety of aeroplanes that RAF service introduced me to, none were more antique or obsolete than the Westland Wapitis with which we were required to defend India's coast. Our five Wapitis, of which two were lost on patrol during the monsoon, were biplanes carrying two 250lb bombs and a swivelling machine gun in the open cockpit. It was a case of *déjà vu*; I was to see something like my childhood biplane memory wheeled out of its tent hangar every day for some months. These old warriors, built in 1929 to a First World War design, were among the oldest to fly in Second Word War. They had been the first to fly over Everest, with the financial aid of Lady Houston in the 1930s. They were much used in the North-West Frontier, bombing bloodthirsty tribesmen, always after warnings. The old brutes (the planes, not the tribesmen) had no brakes, and required ground assistance from two men holding the wing-tips to turn round at the end of the runway. Thank goodness I was never called upon to fly in one. For backups we had a de Haviland Rapide (DH86) airliner converted to carry two bombs, and some Tiger Moths, unarmed. With this assorted Armada regular patrols were flown over the Indian Ocean where Japanese submarines were active, as far as the Laccadive Islands, 200 miles west.

In the intervals of a hectic life, I fell in love with Malabar, its impenetrable mantle of green, its sandy beaches where fishermen shot their nets from primitive canoes, its people all in white, living in thatched huts among the palms, each with its limpid pool. Other fishermen plied their trade from the dipping nets strung on palm-log platforms along the harbour mouth and the beaches of Vypeen Island opposite. White churches, monasteries and Christian schools lay among the palms all around the vast shallow harbour. From the 'cushy berth' of the Malabar Hotel where officers were at first billeted while our brick-built bungalow barracks were constructed, we watched the 'wallums', clumsy great cargo canoes covered in palm-leaf 'tatti' drift lazily by, under tattered sails or by pole-power, while steamers negotiated the deep channel to the docks. Cochin epitomised the historic growth of colonialism, for in this town Vasco de Gama had died in 1524 and was at first buried, until 14 years later when his body was transferred to Belem Convent in Lisbon. His tombstone remains in Cochin's cathedral.

After the Portuguese came the Dutch, who bequeathed their fort to the British. Each left its stamp of churches, schools, hospitals, law and justice (this last including the Inquisition); but failed to make much impression on the indigenous religions. The positive legacy of education, however, left Cochin State and its neighbour Travancore with the highest literacy rate in India. Before the war it was reckoned as 25 per cent; today it is close to 100 per cent.

Although the war was at a critical stage with India under threat of invasion through Burma and its coasts surrounded by hostile fleets, including submarines which preyed on shipping, there was still a peaceful atmosphere about Cochin. We made good use of our spare time by exploring the quaint old Portuguese–Dutch town and fort. Landing on the mainland from the island-airfield, rickshaw-wallahs clamoured for our custom and, picking up the shafts trotted gaily through the narrow streets with their *godowns* exuding the scents of tea, coffee, coconut oil and spices, over the grassy *Maidan* where cricket was played, or into outlying villages where we watched the manufacture of ropes, mats, and all the many uses of coir, the product of the coconut. Sometimes we took a canoe across the shallow lagoons which extend down the coast for hundreds of miles into Travancore State (now part of Kerala), dotted with towns and villages, all under the canopy of coconut palms which makes Malabar one of the most photogenic areas of India. Once our Mess Bearer, a very intelligent man, invited me to visit his village home where his wife and several immaculately dressed children served from their thatched hut a delicate Sunday afternoon tea. On a weekend leave after the monsoon, when the war had quietened down to stalemate, he accompanied me by local buses right down to Cape Comorin, India's southernmost point. Here the fishermen brave the ocean in canoes which are no more than giant logs lashed together.

A few hundred pounds invested in Airship Industries brought a shareholder's discounted flight over London, giving vertical views of the Tower and Parliament, and oblique views of Buckingham Palace. One could walk about in the roomy cabin, but the motion would not suit a bad sailor, being rather similar to that on a small boat in a gentle swell. Unfortunately the company disappeared from a City quote, though it continued to manufacture and market airships in America for a time. One of my most expensive investments: I wonder who got away with the lolly? But it was worth it, for my grandson enjoyed the flight too.

And that about sums up my aerial experience, except for one which *might* be ranked aerial. In Moscow's Park of Rest and Culture, which dispensed leisure diversions for the *hoi polloi*, the foot soldiers of communism (the others had their *dachas*), I rashly committed myself to making a parachute jump from

13

a tower. Having transferred my camera to the Intourist guide to record the historic event, I made a botch of the landing, and sprained my ankle, thus getting a view of the Soviet National Health Service, which was surprisingly good – for tourists at least. A lady doctor came immediately to my hotel and bandaged me up. Joseph Stalin would have been proud of her – for a time at least. This was 1938.

Up to 1942 I was just a snapshotter with any old camera. It was in Cochin that I fell in love with the Rolleiflex, and have used many varieties of them ever since. The basic model is a square box with two lenses – one for viewing and one for taking the picture. I bought one, for £12, from my CO, Squadron Leader Wilfred Russell, and from that moment my education in photography really started. Russell gave me basic drill on the controls: aperture, speed, focus, depth of field, exposure control from the inbuilt exposure meter, all of which were then a mystery to me.

At first I found it strange to be looking *down* into the camera's 2¼-inch square screen in which the scenery appears like a brilliantly-illuminated picture. I am convinced that it is just this feature of the twin lens reflex, which forces you to see the finished picture as it will appear, that makes the best training in photography. It avoids the 'point and shoot' casual attitude which is the cause of so many disappointing results. I have also used many 35mm cameras such as the Nikon which have their own merits such as lightness, but for professional work I am never without my faithful old 'Rollei'.

4

Commanding a Skeleton

*In India everything is done differently
from the rest of the world.
Nothing will ever change this.*

Babur,
The first Moghul Emperor.

It was 1943 and the imminent threat of invasion had receded, at least from the sandy coasts of the Bay of Bengal. But there was an airfield, an RAF Station, and even (hush-hush) a radar station on a nearby hill, always referred to as an AMES (Air Ministry Experimental Station). Vizag, as it was always known, was a stopover on the route between Madras and Calcutta, and was held in readiness for swift reinforcement in case invasion loomed again by sea. The Japanese attempt to invade India through Assam in the north-east came much later.

Hence it was decreed by the Powers that Be that there should be created a Unit, designated 'Skeleton Ops Room', and that Flight Lieutenant Dickins should be its Commanding Officer. There was a complement laid down: of two officers, three Sergeants, three Corporals of clerical grade to file the paper work, coloured forms and signals, and six Enrolled Followers. These last characters, peculiar to the Army in India, were not RAF or IAF personnel, but 'enrolled' from far and wide all over India for any kind of menial work – excluding of course hygiene matters which were the preserve of casteless sweepers. The Followers' pay was Rs.10 a month.

One day out of the blue came a signal from Group HQ requesting that the CO of Skeleton Ops Room should submit an up-to-date record of the 'history' of his unit. This sounded so like a joke, and so busy were we with routine jobs that it was ignored. Some months later an impassioned signal from Bangalore exhorted us to 'expedite history of Skeleton Ops' and berated me for holding up the history of the war. I was tempted to reply in the hallowed words of Wellington in the Peninsular War, that 'If I were to attend to half the drivel that emanates from Your Lordships' office, I should have no

15

time for the business of war'. But prudence restrained me. I wonder if, had I been one of the 'cheeky chappies' brigade, and given Group a saucy answer, it might have bettered my career. I might even have received promotion. It was often thus. But I was a sobersides, and played everything by the book.

If Vizag was a backwater during the two hot weathers and two monsoons that I was stationed there, it had its day of fame some months before. The Indian Air Force's No. 2 Coast Defence Flight, commanded by Squadron Leader David Small, had only just moved from Calcutta to Vizag, where they were lodged in tents near the gravel airstrip. One of the faithful old Wapitis (maximum speed 85 knots) was on patrol with an Indian pilot named Barker, and David as navigator, when they spotted a large Japanese force, consisting of a battleship, an aircraft carrier, a cruiser and two destroyers, in the process of shelling a merchantman. Climbing to 8,000ft, the Wapiti crew shadowed this force, and saw below them two Japanese Zeroes flying towards the coast. Attack was out of the question; reconnaissance was the objective, and normally they would have radioed back to base, but their radio was not working. So they flew low over Andhra University which was Army HQ, and dropped a message.

The same crew took off again to check on the latest position, and finally after dark, determined to drop their two 250lb bombs on the enemy. It was David versus Goliath, but fortunately for him, he could not find the fleet again. After a total of 15 flying hours, he ought to have received a gong – but nobody cared. Coastal Command was unknown in India, and organisation was skeletal, since our convoy of reinforcements, destined for Singapore, had only just arrived in India instead, missing POW status by two months.

David, who was a businessman in Cochin pre-war, and had joined the Coast Defence Force as a civilian flyer, much like our University Air Squadrons, was my CO and one of my best friends at Vizag. Sadly, he met his end the next year when flying a Hudson. Inexplicably, they were seen to jettison their bombs, then plunge into the Bay of Bengal. Nothing was ever found.

The town of Vizagapatam acquired an ignominious reputation on the same day as David's adventure with the Japanese fleet. The harbour was bombed, causing little damage but an almighty panic. A mystery which has never been solved is how people knew about the raid in advance, for the exodus began *before* the first bombs were dropped. The Madras Mail reported: 'Out of a population of 75,000, barely 25,000 were left in Vizagapatam before anything had happened. Soon after the raids, the population had thinned down to 2,000. Essential labour and most of the directing staff of the Municipality and the power house left. But Mr V.E. Lazarus, the Divisional Electrical Engineer, worked heroically with one faithful assistant for 16 hours, doing the stoking himself'.

Anything to break the boredom was welcome at Vizag. With about 300 men on the station, housed in palm-leaf 'tatti' huts right among the thatched huts of *Harijans* (casteless) villagers, and a fluctuating 12–15 officers, daily routine work kept us pretty busy. In the early days there was the chore of censoring mail by hurricane lamps which attracted all the flying objects. Occasional breaks by truck to Waltair, Vizag's beach, for a bathe; there is now a luxury Taj Hotel there. One night there actually was a Japanese raid; the intruder was reported by AMES and clearly heard above us as we scanned the skies by moonlight, and despatched a night-fighting Beaufort, which happened to be on the station, but we saw nothing. The bombs were dropped harmlessly in some sugar cane miles away. Not so funny was the crash of a Wellington in the sea about 15 miles away. Seven out of the eight crew got out and swam ashore to a village, where we rescued them by truck the next day. The eighth man, or what the sharks had left of him, was brought in by ten faithful villagers (who were each rewarded with ten rupees) and delivered to the Mess on a bullock cart, just as we were entertaining the Navy at a very considerable party.

Among the many and varied acts of folly by our rulers was the panic attempt to reinforce Singapore so late that the battle was already lost, condemning thousands of untrained soldiers, airmen and Australians to captivity and often death. I was so untrained that it was not until returning home in late 1944 that I was sent to undergo a course of navigation for Operations Rooms. Yet the first thing I was ordered to do in India was to build an Ops Room – from nothing – and equip it with all the necessary forms and signals equipment for action. Fortune smiled on me when we left Greenock in February 1942, for we had endured no more than a week's gales in the Atlantic before we knew that Singapore had fallen; so we were safe, apart from the submarine menace for two months. And we had drunk the ship dry before Durban; gin and orange at 6d. a glass, with the Warsaw Concerto always ringing in our ears from the Tannoy. And chess; three-handed chess, or *Kriegspiel*.

My sixtieth birthday marked the end of a reel in the movie of life, and the next reel opens with a journey.

REEL 2

The Transformation Scene – A Journey

5

The Journey that set me free

Must I not serve a long apprenticehood
To foreign passages, and in the end,
Having my freedom, boast of nothing else
But that I was a journeyman to grief?

Shakespeare, *Richard II*

Considering all the places in the world which have become 'no go' by reasons of terrorism or nationalism (often the same), it almost seems as if a trail of malevolent influences has followed my travels. I visited Uganda before Idi Amin, Kenya before Mau Mau (or Osama bin Laden), Prague before the Russian tanks rolled in, Peking before the Tian an Men massacre, Cyprus a month before the Turkish Army invaded, Yugoslavia (many times) before it became the last stronghold of a communist bigot, Cambodia before Pol Pot turned the clock back to Year Zero, Persia before the Shah was forced to abdicate, dying of cancer, Burma before Aung San Suu Kyi was put under house arrest and not allowed to see her dying husband, Afghanistan before the Taliban forbade education for women, Sierra Leone before sundry individual revolutions, Ceylon before the Tamil Tigers with their suicide bombers who killed Rajiv Gandhi, and Peru before the 'Shining Path' guerillas, followers of Mao.

Coupled with the unsolved and perhaps unsolvable log-jams of Kashmir, Israel, the Balkans, Central Africa, Iran, Iraq, Syria, Libya, Irian Jaya, Quebec, it would be easy to despair at this naughty world. But why bother?

Ninety-two years teach one to look back as well as into the future. In my childhood I remember the massacres in 'Asia Minor' as Turkey was then called. Armenians, Greeks and Turks all suffered in turn. Go back further, and travel in India was made unsafe by the cult of Kali, the Hindu 'thugs' – until they were put down by Colonel Sleeman, and memsahibs could again travel safely alone with their native bearers. Even between my two wars, ferry ships in the Far East were built with fortified bridges to protect the officers from being hijacked by pirates among the deck passengers. This is not unknown in

21

the Malacca Strait today, boarding by high speed launches. *Plus ça change.* Or 'SNAFU' (Situation Normal, All Fouled Up) as we described cock-ups in the last war.

The truth is that the world has always been equipped with the same proportion of greedy, wicked or stupid people; and of course a much larger proportion of decent, normal people. The only difference in the modern world is that massacres are done with bombs, swindles with computers, and pirates keep their loot in Swiss Bank accounts, not on desert islands. After all, Sir Francis Drake was a very successful pirate. In the old days, the races lived according to their traditions, the *karma* with which the Hindu recognises his caste. With modern science and education, we have less excuse for the idiocies of today.

So, with as much youthful enthusiasm as could be summoned up at a sober 60, I embarked in September 1967 on the journey that set me free. To take an air-conditioned coach from London to Calcutta can be regarded as luxury travel, and so it was, up to a point. It was marketed as 'Adventure Travel' which it also was. Such tours have been run for many years, in both directions, and are much favoured by backpackers from Australia and New Zealand, bent on a spell in the 'mother country'. *En route*, rooms are shared and hotels are moderate to say the least. Our coach, with refrigeration for drinks (which was never used until it blew up in the desert) carried 45 passengers with a driver and courier. We also carried camp beds and sleeping bags for everyone, in case of emergencies. In Europe our hotels were pre-booked from previous experience. Once we crossed the Bosphorous into Asia and relied on telegrams sent a day or two before, life became a little more fraught because sometimes the telegrams did not arrive. Then out came the camp beds, and a search often in darkness for a resthouse or meeting hall.

Our ages were mainly youthful, with a leavening of the mature. The oldest was 67, so at 60 I was an 'oldie'. Only one passenger, a young man from the flat polders of Holland, chickened out, becoming so upset at discovering mountains and hills with hairpin bends, that he quit the tour at Delphi, on the grounds that 'the bus is too long for these narrow roads'. Overnight stops usually followed a run of 300 miles or so, though noteworthy tourist centres such as Venice, Athens and Istanbul rated an extra day for sightseeing. It was a well planned tour, but gremlins sometimes intervened to give us unscheduled delays for repairs.

The calm autumn-tinged scenery of the Rhine and the Neckar, the wooden chalets and mountains of Bavaria and the Tyrol, swept by our picture windows as we crossed the Brenner Pass, with its newly-built elevated bridges and viaducts, into Italy and across the Po Valley to Venice. After saluting the Lion of St Mark, once the major power of the Mediterranean, viewing the Doge's Palace and sampling the overpriced coffee on the Piazza, it was on through the then peaceful Yugoslavia and Bulgaria to Athens. We arrived soon after Jawaharlal Nehru's death, and the Evzones on guard duty at the unknown warrior's tomb carried their rifles reversed. Observing this, an American lady tourist asked, 'Why are they carrying their guns upside down?' It's because they are in mourning, she was told. 'Gee, then what do they do in the afternoon?' she queried. A brief look over the Acropolis, then unfettered by restrictions, led to a merry night of ouzo, bouzouki, song and dance in the crowded tavernas of the Plaka.

Our first encounter with reluctance to provide towels or blankets occurred in a Salonika hotel. Later in Iran a hotel towel was a concession to be won, often to be shared between five or six of us, and always showing many weeks of unwashed service. Hotels too changed character as we moved east; sometimes modern motels but descending to *caravanserais* that had changed little since the days when Marco Polo had joined the camel caravans of traders pioneering the Silk Route, which we were following, to the riches of Asia. *Caravanserais* were square walled compounds where the animals were unloaded, while the travellers sought comfort in small rooms built into the four mud walls. Numbers sharing a room rose from two or three to five, seven, eight; once eleven girls in a dormitory. Foot-level sanitation became the norm. Discomfort, if it cannot be cured, must be endured.

Turkey was a gentle introduction to Asia, sufficiently westernised not to be a culture shock. Thanks to the modernising reforms of Mustafa Kemal, the soldier who replaced the decadent Sultans of the Caliphate at the end of the First World War, the fez was abolished by law; western garb and education for women became the norm. Passing the barracks of Scutari where Florence Nightingale ministered to the wounded of the Crimean War and fought the abysmal ignorance and negligence of the medical profession, we struck west to the ruins of Troy where a gigantic wooden mock-up of the Trojan Horse reminds visitors of their ancient history.

Then it was up onto the Anatolian Plateau for the capital Ankara, a garden city where Ataturk's modern mausoleum is guarded by sentries from three services with queer horizontal leg-raising turns aping those of Greece's Evzone guards.

In Turkey's agricultural east the road climbed often to 6,000 feet, passing grain and grapes laid out to dry, sometimes on the road. There were tempting stops at *chai-khanahs*, simple pavilions with tables and rugs for seating, overlooking river valleys ablaze with poplars in their full autumn glory of gold. At Urgup we feasted on borek, bamias and baklava, the Turkish cuisine which ranks third in my esteem after French and Chinese.

Goreme is a troglodyte village first settled by the early Christians fleeing from persecution. In a steep valley of volcanic tufa they excavated their houses, monasteries and churches, deep in the cliff with windows and balconies and secret passages that could be blocked by a rolling stone. They painted their churches with religious frescos, secure, they hoped, from prying eyes. At Nevsehir there are seven layers of underground houses. Erosion of the porous rock has left many weirdly-shaped chimneys, like giant versions of French pepper-pot roofs, often truncated to a sharp point and topped by a flat cap of harder rock, precariously balanced on the pinnacle.

At Urgup a 'folk dance' was laid on for us; just four beefy men who, after they had given one formal dance, grabbed everyone and started a conga line round the café. The evening became fun, and when one of the party grasped some bells hanging from the roof, it pulled out a light fitting which fused the lights, so it all ended as a drunken Turkish romp.

Further east, villages of mud houses had haystacks on the roof and cow dung plastered on the walls for fuel, as in India. We crossed the Euphrates not far from the site of Alexander's crucial battle of Arbela in the Babylonian valleys, which are perhaps the location of the dawn of civilisation – until somebody comes up with an older candidate. Soon we reached Erzerum, the last town in Turkey, from which we could see Mount Ararat (17,600ft) on the border of Soviet Armenia. Did Noah really land the Ark on Ararat?

It had taken us nine days to get through Turkey, of which two were spent in Istanbul. There were few big towns after Ankara. Kayseri and Malatya stood out, but mostly it was a rural landscape where hirsute men and baggy-trousered women tended herds of cattle, sheep, goats, buffaloes and a few horses. In late October the sun set at 4 p.m. and we often arrived after dark at our overnight motel, which however small was invariably called a 'Palas'. Always we ate well, a great improvement on Greece in this respect.

6

Under the Rule of the Prophet

*And the end of the fight is a tombstone white, with
the name of the late deceased,
And the epitaph drear, 'A fool lies here who tried to
hustle the East'.*

Kipling, *The Naulakha*

The first town in Persia (I prefer the old-fashioned and poetic name to 'Iran') was Maku, really a village, set in a deep gorge under cliffs which had contained cave houses. A gilt statue of the Shah stood in a central fountain, brightly illuminated with coloured lights, in preparation for the coronation ceremonies due in a few days' time. Here the motel had not received our telegram requesting 47 beds, and we had to drag out our camp beds and sleeping bags. I was lucky to get a bed to myself; three other men were three-up in a double. For washing and teeth-cleaning there was no alternative to the roadside ditches of running water which are a feature of all Persian towns and villages.

At our next stop, Tabriz, famous for its carpets, we were soon to be made aware that we were under the rule of Islam. Two of our young girls, who wore the briefest of miniskirts, insisted on going out sightseeing alone, despite our stern warnings. They did not get far. Inevitably their appearance caused a near riot. They were mobbed, and had to be rescued by the police and brought back to our hotel to change into something less inviting to a lascivious Muslim's mind. This had nothing to do with the Mullahs, to whom women have no other purpose than to satisfy men's lusts. At that time (1967) the *chador* or *burkha* had not been imposed by Khomeini's religious police. As in Turkey, Persian women were nominally free; and in fact many dressed – if they could afford it – in the height of western fashion.

The hotel at Tabriz had been modern and clean (except for the towel) but our next stop, Kazvin, was our introduction to the *caravanserai*, a tree-shaded courtyard with rooms around the square. Fair enough, and appropriate to Asia, but the WCs were built with glass tops, leaving occupants visible.

Bedding and towels were indescribably filthy; there was one basin and tap for each line of rooms; and by the morning the WCs were blocked. Toilet paper is not much used in Asia: they prefer water.

We were promised a two-day seaside holiday at Ramsar, and on the way we were shown the perils of the road, meeting two crashes within five miles. On a flat plain, a truck was upside down, the occupants killed. We gave two policemen a lift for a few miles. Then a bus and a truck had met head on. The truck had a load of tomatoes, which turned the road into a gory mess.

Ramsar was indeed a delightful resort on the Caspian Sea, a casino and the Shah's summer palace bespoke its bourgeois elegance; luxury villas stood in gardens of palms, bananas, oranges, jasmine, and European flower-beds. The modern motel had no restaurant, but it was no hardship to stroll up the avenue to the Grand Hotel, next to the Shah's palace, for excellent meals. We had earned a break. There was a long beach, and a fishing port for the caviar-bearing sturgeon which form a major industry. Tea is another; and we visited the local tea factory.

Climbing through forests to the central plateau on which Tehran stands at 3,700ft, higher than Snowdon, we were overlooked by the snow-tipped peaks of the Elburz range, reaching 18,000ft. Fine skiing was enjoyed (at this time) by Persia's middle class as well as the Shah's international fast set. Roads were modern and clean, passing the great lake formed by the Karadj Dam, which is a tourist resort, with a yacht club, water skiing, and summer bungalows.

A fine new toll road approached Tehran, but was not available to trucks and coaches. Factories started to appear, including Leyland and many foreign firms, leading to the central broad tree-lined avenues, as modern as any great city, but still retaining water channels running down each side of the roads.

Tehran divides into two parts; the modern planned city and the old bazaars of crowded lanes, courtyards, teeming cavernous merchants' hovels, exotic carpet shops, ambulating stalls of pomegranates and luscious melons, cosy *chai-khanahs* where men smoke the hubble-bubble, occasional mosques and *medressehs* (Islamic schools), and modern western hotels. Suburbs extend for many miles up the foothills of the Elburz, as the expanding population seeks relief from the extremes of climate. Temperatures vary from −16°C (3°F) in January and February, to 43°C (110°F) in July and August. Tehran's population has expanded from 300,000 in 1950 to in excess of 4 million.

When we arrived, shortly before the Shah's coronation, all towns and villages were *en fête* with ceremonial arches, flags and lavish coloured light displays. So extreme were these that the drain on electricity made the lights so dim that some hotels topped up their lighting with pressure lamps. The pressures on hotel accommodation left scant chance of our finding enough rooms. Some 20 beds were found; then a cellar was pressed into use, after being cleaned following a wedding reception. Here both sexes were crammed together on our six-inch high stretchers, almost touching each other. We got to bed about 3 a.m., and during the night, after lights out, a female voice could be heard to cry out, 'What the devil are you up to!'

For myself, unwilling to make myself uncomfortable for a second night, I accepted an offer of a luxurious suite that was too expensive for most of our intrepid explorers to stomach. With a fellow epicure we paid four guineas (£4.20) each for bed and breakfast (ten shillings, or 50p, was our more usual cost in Asia), and also enjoyed a splendid dinner, the cost of which I was past caring.

An unusual feature, common to all Persian towns, is the *Zurkhaneh*, literally The House of Strength, a sort of physical training society for PT enthusiasts. There are said to be 21 such societies in Tehran alone. In the basement of the Bank Melli Iran, about 20 well-muscled men, bare-chested and wearing nothing but embroidered leather breeches tied at the knee, demonstrated their gymnastics. The ceremony is highly stylised and formal, perhaps like a violent version of *t'ai chi*, with perhaps a Shia religious basis. The exercises are monitored by a leader who marks time, and begin with the men lying on the floor, simulating swimming. They carry boards with which they flex their arms 220 times. Then lying on their backs they raise wooden shields weighing 130lbs each. Most spectacular is the exercising with *mils*, Indian clubs weighing from 30 to 60lbs which they twirl around their heads in precise control. They end with an exercise using a heavy iron bow and chain, involving spinning like a dervish with arms extended.

Elsewhere I met a real dervish in a *chai-khanah*, but did not have the luck to witness the spinning in a trance which can go on for hours. This particular character was regarded as a 'wise man' who offered advice on marital or other personal problems – in effect, a fortune teller. Recently a Persian friend in London recognised him from my photograph.

At the Shah Mosque with its twin minarets, mosaic tiles, and pool in front, people were washing before praying. The Sepahsalar Mosque was more peaceful, its fine archway and minarets set in a garden of shady trees and a large round pool. The exteriors of the Shah's Marble Palace and the Golestan Palace could be photographed, but not the interiors, for all was set for the coronation.

Nine years later when I revisited Persia for a more leisurely tour as a guest of the Government Tourist Office, the Golestan Palace was open, including the magnificent throne room, a long arched cavern with massive crystal chandeliers. The throne itself, on a raised platform in an alcove covered in crystal, glass and mirrors that scintillates with myriad points of reflected light, is perhaps a replica, not the original Peacock Throne which was brought back from Delhi as booty from a sacking and looting sortie made by Shah Nadir, who sat on the throne of the King of Kings in 1736.

The throne itself contains 5,000 jewels, but these are dwarfed by the sphere of solid gold weighing 75lbs, decorated with 51,000 precious stones. These baubles, which in 1976 constituted backing for the nation's currency, were on view in a vault of the Bank Markazi, amidst avalanches of loose, uncut diamonds, rubies, emeralds, turquoises, topazes, garnets, lapis lazuli and pearls which lie in casual heaps in their glass cases. What, one wonders, does all this wealth mean to the present-day Mullahs, who despise personal adornment and conceal all women in black and restrict them from all educated activities? Does it remain, propping up their infamous regime?

The next stage of our journey, of about 250 miles to Isfahan, was mainly through desolate deserts, with a few mud-house villages, and many *qanats*, those ingenious underground water-carrying canals which bring the precious fluid from the mountains to irrigate the desert. They originated many centuries ago, and are maintained today. The only evidence of them above ground are the excavations every few miles, to give access for maintenance through an open well. A lunch stop at a wayside *chai-khanah* in an orchard brought a surprise: electricity, a fridge, tap water, and a splendid lunch of stewed meat and rice – cost, 15p!

Isfahan was always a prize to be cherished, and by none more than Shah Abbas the Great. At the time of our first Queen Elizabeth he made it the capital of the Persian Empire whose history retreats into the mists of time. The city lay on the route of the all-conquering Mongol hordes who swept through Asia to the gates of Vienna, but it miraculously escaped destruction by Genghis Khan, though his descendant Timur the lame (Tamerlane) indulged in a spot of pillage.

As an oasis in the centre of a desert, enjoying a pleasant climate at 4,600ft above sea level, Isfahan is one of the world's great planned cities, astride a river which is spanned by three ancient bridges, each a work of art. The Sharestan, the oldest, goes back to the third century, though much restored. The Bridge of 33 Arches, named after Allahverdi Khan, Shah Abbas's Commander-in-Chief who built it, is made of brick on stone pillars; and at the Shah's express request rooms were built into it for the convenience of travellers, where performances took place and marriages were celebrated. The third bridge, the Khaju, has similar features, and is even more used for picnicking in the summer in the painted pavilions which line it. It functions also as a weir, for the sluices between pillars can be blocked to control the flow of water. Like the Moghul Emperor who inscribed over a bridge in the Shalimar Gardens in Kashmir 'The world is a bridge; pass over it but build no house thereon', the Khaju bridge bore poetic inscriptions reflecting Islamic (and Buddhist) philosophy.

Everything in Isfahan is on the grand scale. The *Maidan* claims to be the largest square in the world. Certainly Shah Abbas played polo on it; the goalposts are still there. Ali Qapu is a six storey gatehouse of the former palace, from the painted music room of which the Shah watched the polo or processions, and looked across to the Sheikh Lutfullah Mosque whose blue mosaics and honeycombed porches are the most exquisite of all. Nearby lies the Shah Mosque (seventeenth century) with its huge cupola of cerulean blue and flanking minarets, representing the head and raised arms of a man at prayer. The Jame or Friday Mosque is one of the oldest, going back to the eleventh century, and its golden *ivans* or porches, which were added later, also have a honeycomb effect. The Madressah (Theological College) of the Shah's mother stands in a courtyard garden of tree-shaded pools, with cupola and minarets of blue and yellow faience. Shafts of sunlight pierce holes in the roof of the bazaar, planned by Shah Abbas, where coppersmiths still hammer out their designs based, like the mosaics, on Arab patterns, reflecting the taboo on representing human or animal forms. In The Chehel Sotun, the Palace of Forty Columns, so called because its mere twenty columns are reflected in the surrounding pool, there are some interesting paintings, including one of Shah Abbas meeting an Indian Moghul Emperor.

The Shah Abbas Hotel, which was converted from an old *caravanserai* by the Iranian National Insurance Company, only two years before out visit, is really sumptuous. Standing in a perfect garden, its interior reflects the ultimate in luxury; a sweeping staircase, and walls painted with traditional Persian flowery themes, but including panels of languorous dancing girls. It was used in a film not long ago; but those girls must have shocked the Mullahs, and it has probably all been vandalised.

Of Isfahan's 400,000 inhabitants, there were 4,000 Jews and 5,000 Armenian Christians. The latter were originally imported by Shah Abbas because of their skilled craftsmanship. They are still present, and their Armenian cathedral in the suburb of Julfa is well worth a visit. They were given special status by the Shah, with the traditional tolerance of Islam, now sadly forgotten in Iran and increasingly elsewhere. The world regresses to the savagery of the Middle Ages. Even Europeans tear each other apart in the Balkans for what is basically a religious, rather than a racial reason. Will we never learn? Probably not.

On 26 October, a holiday as Coronation Day, there were great crowds, and a miliary parade on the *Maidan*, with officious police chivvying people around, but an Army Captain was kind enough to conduct me up the narrow winding stairs to the highly decorated music room of the Ali Qapu Palace, from the balcony of which Shah Abbas used to view proceedings on the Maidan.

Leaving Isfahan two days later for another 200-mile run to Shiraz, we had not gone far when an oil leak developed in a pump, and we had to return for a fractured aluminium base to be welded. This lost us a day, but I can't think of a better place for a wasted day than Isfahan.

Rising at 4.45 a.m. for an early start next day, the route included a stop for the historic site of Persepolis, undoubtedly one of the Seven (man-created) Wonders of the World, Our delayed schedule allowed only two hours to cover the site; but I worked so fast that I took almost as many pictures as on a later proper visit, with overnight stay nearby, in 1976.

The royal palace of Darius III, Lord of the Persian Empire whose two and a half millennia of history were celebrated by Shah Mahomed Reza Pahlavi in 1970, was destroyed by fire when conquered by Alexander the Great in 330 BC It emerged from its long sleep under the sands of the desert in a remarkable state of preservation. Though only pillars remain of the stately halls, arches and gateways, the ground plan, walls, staircases and many statues are intact, in pristine condition. We walked up the giant staircase where ambassadors from 28 nations, from as far afield as India, Central Asia, Greece and Ethiopia, had mounted to the Apadana where Darius received their tribute. On the walls, low-relief friezes showed men in the garb of their race, bearing typical products of their country: a lamb, a horn of oil, bales of cloth, all in perfect detail.

Pairs of figures march side by side up the steps, sometimes turning to speak to the man behind, or holding hands. The perspective is precise, though the depth of stone is only about three inches. As *trompe'l-oeil* it is artistic genius – historically it is explicit and accurate.

Before Islam invaded, the Persians were Zoroastrians, believers in the supreme god Ahura Mazda, whose image is represented in the sacred fire which is worshipped in fire temples tended by priests. Like the Parsis of India (who came from Persia) they put out their dead on Towers of Silence, where they are speedily disposed of by vultures. Survivors of the Zoroastrian religion are centred at Yezd in the desolate Great Southern Desert; our night stop a few days later. Here tall chimneys provide many houses with a cooling draught to underground rooms where inhabitants shelter from the scorching summers.

After Isfahan there was still another thousand miles to go, across the Great Southern Desert, to Zahedan on the Pakistan frontier. Kerman, of carpet fame, was another night stop; a *caravanserai* with four in a room, in soggy beds, two WCs for all, which soon blocked, and the usual difficulty of getting any towels at all; clean ones are not expected. Never mind! There was a good dinner, and most of us had a bottle of Persian vodka or Greek brandy, both of which were cheap.

Our visit to Persepolis gave me seriously to think. Satisfactory though it is to chalk up an ambition fulfilled, travel teaches that the more you see of the world, the more it shows you how much you *don't* know, haven't seen. Slowly the plot advanced to 'doing it my way'. Future reels to unwind included the pyramids of Egypt, the Great Wall of China, the Inca city of Macchu Picchu, the buried Khmer city of Angkor Wat, the Shwe Dagon Pagoda of Rangoon, the Buddhist temple of Borobudur in Java, the Aztec pyramids of Mexico, the Shinto and Buddhist temples of Japan. It took another 30 years, but all slotted into my pattern of life – of moving pictures – eventually. After all, I was only 60.

Thinking of the ancient civilisations, of which we in the west are largely ignorant, is a little humbling. Europeans thought that Marco Polo and a few brave explorers 'discovered' Mongolia and China. Christopher Columbus was admired because he overcame the fear, common among fifteenth-century seamen, of falling off the edge of the world if they ventured too far west of Cape Verde. The Portuguese navigators (Vasco de Gama *et al.*) were hailed for their bravery in rounding the Cape of Good Hope, in search of the spices which they knew came from the Far East, but by a long and expensive overland route. As for Darkest Africa, they were still searching for the source of the Nile in Victoria's time, but the great stone palace in Zimbabwe had been built centuries before.

And what were the Chinese doing all this time? They cared not a fig for the barbarian western world, but they were inquisitive enough to send the eunuch Admiral Cheng Ho, with a fleet of 300 huge junks, on expeditions of discovery across the Indian Ocean, to the East African coast, a century before Vasco de Gama reached India in 1498.

In 1793 (only 45 years before my Grandpa was born), King George III sent a mission under Lord Macartney to Emperor Chien Lung (Qianlong), seeking to establish diplomatic relations and a modicum of trade. It was done in the grandest style, with lavish presents of the latest scientific instruments, a magnificent coach and a team of horses to match. Enormous expense demonstrated the importance attached to bringing China into the comity of western nations. It was all in vain. After two visits extending over three years, the noble lord was sent away with a flea in his ear, and the official answer: 'Our Celestial dynasty, which sways the wide world, attaches no value to the costly presents which are offered at Our Court: what we appreciate is the humble spirit of the offerers. We have commanded our Viceroy (in Canton) to accept in order that your reverence may be duly recognised' (Alain Peyrefitte's, *The Collision of two Civilisations*).

The Emperor had a point. Think of any modern invention you like, and in almost all cases (excepting nuclear power which is nothing to be proud of), the Chinese had something that did the job almost as well, long before. The list of Chinese inventions that forestalled the West is endless. Computers? They had the abacus.

Such weighty thoughts were hardly in the minds of our party of adventurers in 1967; nor in my mind as a visiting journalist in 1976, when the Shah's rule seemed secure, and Iranian tourism was on the upward trend. The rumble of popular dissent was underground, and it was a surprise to most when a mainly student-led plot exploded into the occupation of the US Embassy in Tehran on 4 November 1979, with the capture of 66 diplomats and guards who endured 454 days of death threats as hostages. America's abortive attempt to rescue them ended in the crashing of helicopters in the desert, ensuring that Carter's presidency ended in farce.

7

Last Lap to Freedom

A canter down some dark defile
Two thousand pounds of education
drops to a ten rupee jezail.

Kipling

By now we were suffering from the corrugated roads and dust which penetrated into everything and caused any biscuits or pills carried on the shelves of the coach to crumble into dust. The coach chassis suffered too, progressive disintegration of the shock absorbers, front and rear, leaving the main springs unchecked, light-heartedly to toss us about, like a barge on an ocean swell. Particularly in the rear seats (which we occupied in rotation) if you hit the roof on the bound, the chances were that you might contact the hard armrest of your seat with your bottom on the rebound. Spare shock absorbers were fitted, twice, but none could stand up to the appalling roads. Riding jockey-like, clutching the back of the seat in front was *de rigueur*.

The big day for our gremlins was 2 November. They launched a concerted attack. First the air-conditioning packed up which was no hardship as it had never been used, but with it went the refrigeration unit which also burst, filling the coach with ammonia fumes, necessitating a rapid exit. Then the windscreen blew in with an explosion, depositing a shower of glass on my lap – I happened to be in the front seat. Finally at 11.25 p.m. the engine decided, temporarily, to stop. It was not until 12.30 a.m. that we reached Zahedan, after 16 hours on the road, each shaken to a jelly.

We were now in the extreme south of Iran, not far from the Trucial Coast of ill repute. Although these little contretemps caused a good deal of grumbling at the time, and some talked of quitting the tour, there was no means of doing so before 'civilisation' at Quetta, and anyway I think we were secretly a bit proud of gritting teeth and overcoming obstacles. Isn't that what Britons are supposed to do?

We were by now quite accustomed to a routine drill. For lunch stops we carried hunks of naan, the flat unleavened bread which is not much harder on

32

the seventh day than on the first, and a bottle of water, which are supplemented with whatever we could pick up at village stalls. A tin of sardines or spam was a treat. As for comfort stops on desert roads with not a bush in sight, they were simply solved. Gents on the right, ladies on the left.

Crossing the Iran–Pakistan border into Baluchistan, formerly a province of India, I felt a lifting of the spirits. I knew where I was when buying a cup of sweet milky char for four annas. They had not yet decimalised the rupee. Border posts were always a source of delay, for passport details of our entire crew had to be listed and translated for the benefit of officials who, with Asiatic regard for routine, struggled to translate our occupations into their own language. Attempting to translate 'assistant railway booking clerk' or 'airline hostess' into Farsi or Urdu was so tedious that eventually the courier gave up. Since manay of our girls were nurses, and some of the Down Under men were sheep shearers, all women became nurses and all men sheep shearers.

After several hours of officialdom, we arrived at Dalbandin at 12.30 a.m., on the Pakistan side. Here we enjoyed one of the best welcomes of the tour. I had already had a snack of rice and dhal at the frontier shack, but to our surprise the *chowkidar* (watchman) at the PWD (Public Works Department) resthouse where our stay had been booked by telegram had actually kept hot for us a meal of chicken, beef and rice, plus stewed apples *and custard*. The rule of the Memsahibs had not been forgotten. Of course a PWD bungalow is only designed for a few touring officials, so it was a case of camp beds again. As we bedded down on the verandah it was one of the happiest nights I remember. The stars shone more brightly than we ever see in England; from Orion rising to the zenith, to Sirius down by the horizon, and the Milky Way sending its soft glow over half the heavens, it was like a stage set. It was quite cold, but I slept fairly well, despite barking dogs and cicadas and a nervous cough from another bed. Rising at 5.30 a.m. with the first orange glow, we were in a sandy grove of palms and casuarinas. Camels were being loaded, and a small crowd of Baluchi elders with long white beards were sitting in a circle and holding a tribal *jirga*.

After washing and shaving in a pool, using the water as a mirror, breakfast followed: porridge (the Memsahibs again) and hard-boiled eggs. Soon we were climbing into the mountains to reach Quetta at 5,508ft. The most important military station in the west of Pakistan, it had been destroyed in the earthquake of 1935, when 20,000 people died in 30 seconds, including many British. At the time my father was head of the Ordnance Department of India in Simla, from which tents, engineers and medical supplies were organised.

With western-style hotels in flowery gardens, and Chinese restaurants, we feasted to make up for lost meals. In the military cantonment I lunched at the club, meeting an English lady whose father was in the Ordnance Corps, like mine. She had been married in Delhi in 1947 and got out just before the rioting erupted. We spent three days in Quetta, seeking spare shock absorbers

– we had already used the spare set we carried. No go. They were ordered from home, despatched to Bombay, and there they remain, bound by the interminable red tape of Indian customs.

Soon it was another frontier, into Afghanistan. The long climb over the Khojak Pass at 7,575ft followed one of Alexander's possible routes where now a strategic railway climbs with the aid of tunnels and viaducts cut from the rocky pass, to end at Chaman. The crossing here took four and a half hours. The most remarkable surprise in Afghanistan was to find ourselves riding on smooth tarmac, wide roads perfectly graded, with culverts bridged and drained by huge metal tunnels. The gift apparently of the USA, while Soviet Russia made the same attempt to curry favour in the north.

Kandahar awakes thoughts of Lord Roberts who led the avenging army after the defeat at Maiwand in 1880; almost a replica of the massacre on the Khyber in 1842. Staying in a pleasant, clean bungalow hotel, I strolled out for dinner in the dark. Hearing eastern music coming from a large house, with a *shamiana* and fine carpets on the steps, I investigated and was invited in. A local police Inspector was holding a wedding feast with a singer and five musicians, including a superb tabla player. Fine faces of hawk-nosed bearded Afghanis with long shirts, waistcoats and floppy white turbans treated me as a guest with traditional Muslim hospitality. 'My house is yours' is a typical greeting. Why have so many Muslims forgotten?

Kabul was a two-night stop, and excited no particular interest, being an orderly city on a river, with modern hotels; the Spinza where we stayed was Bulgarian-owned. There was the Bala Hissar, the fort where Macnaugten the British Envoy was murdered as the prelude to the retreat and murder of the entire British army and its thousands of 'followers', from which a single survivor, Doctor Brydon, struggled through some weeks later. Lady Sale, one of the surviving women who was spared, recounts vividly what was probably Britain's greatest military disaster. For the Russians, a century and a half later, they were lucky to get out when they did. *Plus ça change.*

Another day, another frontier, and after another four hours of pen-pushing, the nurses and sheep shearers were permitted to cross the Khyber Pass into Peshawar in Pakistan. From here on, we were in the atmosphere of the Raj (only 20 years deceased) with western-style hotels and the temptation of delicious curries. Paradoxically, only after surviving weeks of dubious messes from boiling cauldrons in desert villages, it was not until the very latest luxury hotel in Lahore, just opened, that the Dragon struck. However, a dose of streptotriad and gallons of lemon tea kept the body mobile for work as usual.

Hitting Alexander's route south from the Hindu Kush, we now had to cross the Indus at Attock. The steel road and rail bridge erected in 1885 to expedite reinforcement of the always troubled North-West Frontier Province, was overlooked by the massive fort built by the Emperor Akbar in 1586. He must have had his frontier troubles too. *Plus ça change.* We stopped to talk to an old retired Jemadar of the 24th Punjabis wearing medals which he proudly displayed. A passer-by translating for us remarked when he saw the medals bearing the effigy of King George VI, 'Ah, he was our King'.

After Peshawar, Rawalpindi where the Memsahibs took the children in the hot weather, and Lahore, Moghul city *par excellence*, where Akbar held court, Jehangir is buried, and Aurangzeb built the Badshahi Mosque, then the largest in the world. Lahore was contested over the centuries by Persians, Afghans and by Ranjit Singh for the Sikhs, as rulers of the Punjab. He built, perhaps as a gesture of defiance from the spoils of Moghul buildings, a marble pavilion which lies provocatively outside the Hazuribagh Darwaza (gateway) of Akbar's fort. No love has ever been lost between Muslims and Sikhs.

The end of the journey was nigh for me. After another exhausting tussle with red tape at the sensitive Pakistan/India frontier at Ferozepore (where my father had once commanded the Army Uniform Factory and learnt all about tailoring), we descended on Amritsar, holy city of the Sikhs. A breakaway from Hinduism, they are a tolerant people. Their traditional hospitality for all of whatever religion provides a free meal and shelter to travellers. Having paid homage to the glorious Golden Temple (which Mrs Gandhi rashly shelled, thus ensuring her own death), islanded in a great pool where the faithful wash, it was time to quit this mode of travel. The discomfort of unchecked springs was positively dangerous and several ladies had been knocked about. So, in a rickshaw and another carrying my baggage, it was down to the railway station to buy a ticket to Delhi and wave goodbye to my surprised mates, who in due course reached Calcutta, but never did reach the advertised destination, Katmandu, for the coach was unable to negotiate the hairpin bends. Bear in mind that it was only after the last war that a proper motor road had been built into Nepal's 4,000–5,000ft average height. The King's Rolls Royce had been carried up in pieces on the backs of hundreds of coolies.

Ye gods! How old it makes me feel to remember that the last time I was in Nepal there were Chinese trolley-buses!

8

Pakistan Beyond the Khyber

When you're wounded and left on Afghanistan's plains
And the women come out to cut up what remains
Just roll to your rifle and blow out your brains
An' go to your Gawd like a soldier.

Kipling, 'The Young British Soldier'

On the press stand for the Armed Forces Parade on Pakistan Day in 1979 there was an uncanny likeness to the Republic Day Parade in New Delhi. The scarlet uniforms and lances of the mounted President's Bodyguard, the state coach (Pakistan got the silver one and India the gold when the Indian Army was divided in 1947), the spit and polish, the meticulous salutes, the starched puggris, loose shirts and baggy pants, all were redolent of the Raj. I stood beside President Zia ul Haq on the saluting base and photographed him in close-up as he solemnly promised elections in November. But as I drove past the prison where his rival, Ali Bhutto languished, I did not take him seriously. Within a few weeks Bhutto was hung by the neck, and in 1988 Zia was no more, assassinated (probably) in a mysterious helicopter crash. Asia's history was continuing to unwind – What little scraps we mortals see of the moving picture!

The land between the Hindu Kush and the Karakorams is the wild North-West Frontier of 8,000-metre mountains, so steep and remote that the only means of transport for anyone too infirm to walk is a basket on the back of another man. This gives rise to the quip 'the Father's basket is for the son'. As recorded by John Keay this means a crude form of euthanasia, when the patriarch being carried up to a suitable high cliff chuckles it to himself.

More blood has been shed over the Khyber Pass than any comparable mountain area. When I first crossed over on the coach trip in 1967 it was at dusk and little could be seen of the grim depths of the defile where a British Army was cut to pieces by Pathan tribesmen in the ignominious retreat of 1842. In 1979, guided by a knowledgeable Mr Khan, I traversed it from Peshawar to the Afghan frontier at Torkham, beyond which I could go no

36

further without a visa. But the sentries on both sides were relaxed and friendly, posing for pictures, and people were crossing quite casually in both directions. Today the temporary peace of a devastated country envelops Afghanistan, but on Pakistan's Indian frontier at Lahore the nervous tension is relieved by the sentries on both sides with a competitive display of military spit and polish of ludicrous extremes. Flags are lowered as the gates clang to, and gigantic Pakistani soldiers, all over 6ft tall, throw their feet above their heads as they march. It's all good fun, appreciated by a small crowd as each side strives to outdo the other in theatrical manoeuvres. Better, as Winston Churchill said, 'to jaw-jaw rather than a war-war'.

Mr Khan was insistent that before leaving the road for photography, I should reconnoitre carefully the surrounding hilltops, from which hawk-eyed tribesmen used to scan the road for movements of British troops or supply wagons. It was still possible that I might be sniped, for Pathans disapprove of foreigners in general and photographers in particular. In the days of the Raj, tactical rules required the Army to establish their own pickets, stone huts or *sangars* to crown every dun-coloured rocky peak, before the Regiment could proceed. In the Tribal Reserves every man carries a rifle, even in the bazaars, and owes allegiance to no one but his tribe; paying no taxes, observing no Pakistani laws beyond the confines of the road. We passed relics of the Raj: the long low Shagai Fort of the Khyber Rifles, and the roadside rock plastered with the badges of British Regiments who had tasted the Frontier life – nasty, brutish and short in all too many cases.

Scores of trucks laden with contraband goods (and drugs) and overflowing with passengers on the garishly decorated roofs plied the route in both directions, while a camel caravan plodded by on rough ground just below. The tax-free regime has awarded a thriving transport monopoly to Pathans, many of whom are very rich. Landi Khotal, the summit town, may be an insanitary dump with open drains, but all kinds of scarce and luxury goods is on sale, and one headman has air-conditioning and refrigeration in his mud-walled compound and blockhouse home.

The railway from Peshawar to the Afghan frontier, which cost £2 million to build its 26 miles in 1920–1925, is an amazing engineering feat, thought impossible at the time, but fully justified for strategic reasons. It has 34 tunnels and 92 bridges, and until recently one steam train a week ran as far as Landi Khotal, of tourist interest – but now even that is no more.

At Darra Adem Khel near Peshawar the tribal arms industry is home-based. Every house is engaged in producing handmade copies of every conceivable weapon, indistinguishable from the original. I was offered and demonstrated anything from a revolver to a Lee Enfield, a Kalashnikov or a bazooka. There was even a neat little pencil which fires real bullets, also home-made. Just the job for a quiet assassination, and it is said of Pathans (not Pakistanis) that they prefer to commit mayhem by trickery rather than in a straight fight. They must have had a field day when Russia challenged history.

When the Soviet Army invaded Afghanistan, it made me laugh because, lacking the experience of the British and Indian Armies in tribal guerilla warfare, their prospective fate was all too obvious. They only lasted a few years, achieving nothing except to set a civil war in motion. Britain, faced with a century of treacherous combat and hardship which for some had a certain mordacious charm, kept a peace of a sort. Pakistan, in contrast, is content to leave the tribes very much to their own devices. This includes the largely unrestricted export of opium and heroin, for with the blatant corruption which permeates Pakistan it is tacitly accepted that few crops will grow so well in the arid soil as poppies.

Poor Russia: she was far too late for the Great Game!

Until late in the nineteenth century, the area of western Kashmir beyond the Indus, known as Dardistan, was *terra ingognita*. A shadowy claim to suzerainty by the Maharajah of Kashmir did little to impede the tribal chieftains in their internecine feuds, when brothers were routinely eliminated as a matter of prudence by every new ruler. The Mirs of Hunza and Nagar, whose shaky kingdoms faced each other across the valley of the Hunza River, were free to pursue their traditional occupation of raiding caravans.

Hunza was proclaimed by travellers until recently as a Shangri-La without crime or money, so I was anxious to meet the Hunzakuts whose famed longevity was attributed variously to their dried apricots and the glacier sediments in their water. Until the Karakoram Highway was built with Chinese labour (and 400 fatalities, roughly one for every mile) to link the headwaters of the Indus with the Chinese province of Sinkiang via the 16,000ft Khunjerab Pass, Hunza could only be reached by 56 miles of fearsome track, at which even a goat might shy. Under towering snow-capped peaks, it is scraped out of sheer walls of friable scree, supported by logs and boulders where gaps occur in ravines. Today, the 400 miles of blacktop highway, broad enough for two trucks to pass anywhere, has removed the romance with the dangers.

I flew from Rawalpindi to Gilgit, a desolate outpost of the Great Game when Russian designs on India were greatly feared, and a British Residency was maintained right up to Independence. The flight is notorious for sometimes involving flying in the Indus gorge below the mountain tops. This day it was clear, and the two pilots of the Fokker Friendship invited me, as an ex-member of the Royal Indian Air Force, to join them on the flight deck. We crossed the Babusar Pass at 12,500ft over a sea of snow and ice, from which Nanga Parbat, the Naked Lady, projected in a pyramid peak. Approaching Gilgit they played a well-worn trick. As we descended into a narrow valley and headed straight for a mountain wall, they asked me, 'Where is the airfield?' 'Find the runway for us; we are lost'. I could see nothing but rock facing us until at the last moment they made a sharp left turn and there round the corner lay the short landing strip.

1938

Left: Wandering musician in
Caucasian village

Right: A poor street in Old Tiflis

Below: Village gossip at Kazbek,
7000 ft elevation on Georgian
Military highway

Left: Mt. Kazbek, 16,545 ft. The
footbridge spans the river Terek

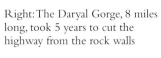

Right: The Daryal Gorge, 8 miles
long, took 5 years to cut the
highway from the rock walls

Cochin's passenger-bomber. Sqdn. Ldr. Wilfred Russell, Flying Officer Rabb

No.5 Coast Defence Flight. A De Haviland Rapide (DH86) 1942

Overflying Willingdon Island with airfield expanding, August 1942

Synagogue built in 1568, Cochin

...min ladies of Suchindrum bathing in the temple tank

Poling a Wallum through the palm-girt backwaters of Cochin

A Catalina lands at Cochin. A fishing canoe ferries the crew ashore

...ny boy
...ench citzen of Mahé, French colony on Malabar coast 1942

Ambulance. Trichinopoly,
cigar manufacturing town, South India 1942

Officers' Mess, RAF Vizagapatam, July 1943. Left to right: Author, Sodhi, Oliver, Godber, Handley, Harries, Dowsett, Griffiths, Byrne, Barfield

Telegu villagers, our next door neighbours, 1943

Dhobi Ghat, our village laundry, 1943

Brenner Pass elevated motorway still under construction in 1967

The Village Band after church service, Pians, Austrian Tyrol

one sentry
mourning for death of Jawaharlal Nehru, Athens 1967

The Acropolis, Athens

Historical Regatta, Venice

Eibhlin in Venice

Cave houses, Goreme, Turkey

Weird erosion, Urgup, Turkey

Family of Qashqa'i. A tribe who live around Shiraz. The women's full skirts are in brilliant colours and topped by gauzy veils

one room, Golestan Palace, Tehran

Carpet weaver, Tehran

khaneh, Tehran

17th century bazaar of Shah Abbas, Isfahan

Jame Mosque entrance, Isfahan.
Women in Chador

Jame Mosque interior. Women
have special quarters

Pol-E-Khaju. Bridge built by Sh
Abbas. The arches, cooled by the
river, are used for recreation

Shah Mosque, Isfahan. Built by Shah Abbas
in 1612

Above: Meeting in the desert. The outward-bound and homeward-bound meet by chance in Iran's Great Southern Desert 1967
Below: Persepolis: Relics of the 2500 year old palace of Darius destroyed by Alexander in 330 B.C.

n attacks a bull

Carrying the throne of Darius

rahminy bull is brought in tribute

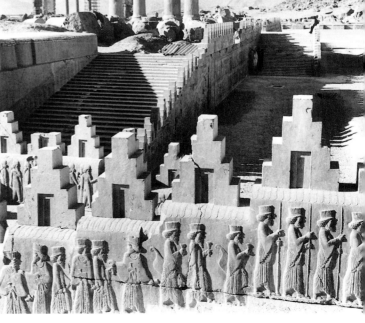

Staircase to the Apadana

The Khyber

Bus travel, Afghanistan

Baluchi elders at a tribal jirga at Dalbandin, Iran–Pakistan border

Badshahi Mosque, Lahore. Built by Moghul Emperor Aurangzeb in 17th century. A pavilion of Ranjit Singh, the Sikh ruler of Punjab, stands in foreground

Bazaar, Rawalpindi

Evening prayers at Mosque of Marhabat Khan, Peshawar

sident Zia-ul-Haq reviewing troops at Rawalpindi, 1979

March past of a Pakistani regiment

Shagai Fort of the Khyber Rifles.

Jamrud Gate. 'Gateway to the Khyber'. A tribesman carries a rifle even when shopping

Gunshop. Darra Adem Khel. Afridi tribal village

Badges of British Regiments who served on the Khyber Pass, with some Pathan schoolboys on the road

western Himalayas. Nanga Parbat

dslide on Karakoram highway falling into the Indus river, this one
rooned me overnight

Main road of the Punial valley running west from Gilgit. This is what
the original road to Hunza was like

Hunzakuts, children of Hunza. Many have blue eyes and red hair. The pillbox hat is worn with veil by all women, and unusually by the boy

Jan Alam, Rajah of Punial. He has 9 brothers and 9 sisters from his father's 3 wives

Wazir Ali Murad, a Hunzakut aged 100½ in 1979

The snow is hardly melted when ploughing must be done (barefoot) for basmati rice. Kashmir

Shikaras at dawn. Dal lake, Srinagar

Houseboat life, Srinagar

The Hookah. He's handsome and he knows it. Kashmir

Fuji-san, over drying paddy

Torii at Toshogu shrine, Nikko

Flyover junction Akasaka district, Tokyo

Chanoyu tea ceremony by a Maiko (Trainee Geisha)

Chanoyu by Kyutaro Moriyama. A tea master (Teacher of the ceremony)

The old Mir of Hunza who welcomed occasional travellers to his castle is dead and his son works in a government office in Islamabad. But the centenarians are still there, and the rosy-cheeked children whose blue eyes and red hair are the legendary relics of Alexander's soldiers. Fruit blossom carpeted the valley and only a day of black clouds hiding Rakaposhi spoilt the experience for a photographer.

A jeep excursion up the Gilgit valley to Punial, a small former independent state, gave a taste of what the old Hunza road was like. The 'road', nowhere more than jeep-width, followed the contours to avoid bridging gullies, and gaps were filled with crumbling dry stone walls. Gradients of 25 per cent led to blind corners, cut out of the cliffs with overhangs, 500ft above the river. A limitless horizon of the snow-capped Karakorams which form the frontier of Russia and Afghanistan, was devoid of trees except for the level banks of the river, where small patches of wheat punctuated thousands of fruit trees.

My local guide, a charming young man named Tariq Wali, was a nephew of the former Rajah of Punial, whose bungalow home we visited in Shirqulah. Rajah Jan Alam, a handsome two metres high, with a black handlebar moustache, wore brown homespun and a flat Chitrali cap. He provided green tea while we ate our picnic lunch. He had nine brothers and nine sisters, from his father's three wives. A keen fisherman, he used to make good wine, but Bhutto stopped all that, he regretted. The Rajah was responsible for administration of his state until 1972, drawing taxes in kind from the villagers – and remitting them in case of hardship. He now drew an allowance of Rs.2500 a month from the Pakistan government, who have put in a District Commissioner, police, schools and dispensaries. This is progress, I suppose? But I wonder. We passed a primitive school *en route*, with the boys squatting outside. Of girls there was no sign. The master, who was Tariq Wali's cousin, carried a shotgun.

As often happens to visitors to Gilgit, bad weather shut down the airfield for several days, leaving no alternative but a jeep ride of 400 miles on the KKH (as the highway is called) to return to Rawalpindi. Starting in the dark at 4 a.m. most of the journey was in pouring rain, hindered by countless landslides semi-blocking the road. At 11 a.m. after 200 miles, all progress was barred by a mass of earth and rocks right across the road and pouring over the edge into the muddy Indus 500 feet below.

It was a dismal prospect until, retracing our steps to the nearest village, we noticed a pucka stone building bearing the sign 'Officers' Mess'. Tariq remembered that he had a cousin serving in the Kohistan Scouts. Soon we were being entertained to tea and biscuits by three young officers until they went to prayers at 2 p.m., and I was shown to a guest room with two beds and a flush toilet. It was 24 hours before the Army bulldozers had cleared the road. While immensely grateful for the hospitality and the curry sent by a batman to my lonely room for dinner, it was a little disappointing not to be invited into the actual mess with Tariq. The enmity which has set two armies of Indians at loggerheads across glaciers in the remotest mountains in the world has created a miasma of fear which paints all foreigners with suspicion. Another of the perverse and illogical results of Partition in 1947.

According to the theory of plate tectonics, the continent of India is being forced northward a few inches every year, causing the Himalayas to buckle; and thus the KKH, which follows the winding gorges of the Indus down to the plains, is so unstable that landslides are a regular feature. A sobering thought: if the figures of six inches a year are correct, as outlined in Professor Keith Miller's *Continents in Collision*, then India has moved 40 feet nearer to China in my lifetime!

So here I am back in the heart of Asia, but my journey's end has only an interval, and now the time of remembrance is shot with a series of flashbacks at two preceding generations.

REEL 3

Action in Reverse: Flashbacks of three generations, two centuries

9

In Grandpa's Footsteps

Japan is essentially a country of paradoxes and anomalies – where all – even familiar things – put on new faces and are curiously reversed.
                    Sir Rutherford Alcock, *The Capital of the Tycoon*

In mid-Victorian times, Japan was ruled, so far as anyone knew, by the Shogun, who had full powers; though there lurked in the background a shadowy and secretive figure, the Mikado, to whom was ascribed divine origin. He appeared to be the supreme ruler, though his sanctity kept him incommunicado in his palace in Kyoto.

The Shogun was no more than the strongest of the feudal lords, the Daimyo who ruled their clan territories. The Tokugawa Ieyasu emerged in 1603 as the ruler whose clan held onto power until the Mikado was 'restored' to power in the civil war that ended in 1868. This was confusing to the western powers who sought to establish contact with Japan, and it was seven years between the signing of treaties by the Shogun to their ratification by the Mikado.

My grandfather, F.V. Dickins, CB, was one of the pioneer Europeans who followed the American Commodore Matthew Perry, who in 1854 sought to open commercial relations with the mysterious country that had been barred to foreigners (except for a handful of Dutch merchants who were allowed to trade in Nagasaki) for two and a half centuries.

The two Far Eastern countries, China and Japan were xenophobic. To the Chinese, all foreigners were Barbarians; to the Japanese they were feared, and strictly excluded from the sacred shores of the Mikado's realm. Japanese were equally debarred, under pain of death, from leaving their country. Christians were especially feared as a menace to the established Shinto and Buddhist religions, and were persecuted in the late sixteenth and early seventeenth centuries by Japanese rulers.

So extreme was the fear of foreigners that if one of the Dutch merchants in Nagasaki on their artificial island of Deshima died he was denied even six feet of Japanese earth in which to be buried. The ocean was his watery grave.

Reciprocal trade with China and Japan became established through the system of Treaty Ports, in which foreigners could reside and enjoy 'extra-territorial rights', meaning that they were exempt from the laws of the country, but would govern themselves according to their own laws. Not always did the foreigners conform to this ideal. In some quarters early settlers were described as 'the scum of Europe'. No doubt there were a few ne'er-do-wells and 'remittance men' among them.

In the nineteenth century the South China Seas were the haunt of pirates, and much violence, typified by Hong Kong and its Opium Wars, attended the establishment of Treaty Ports around the coast of China. In Japan it was rather different. Commodore Perry's two visits, in 1853 and 1854 with his fleet of menacing black ships secured entry without firing a shot or losing a man. Formal treaties followed in 1858 for the USA, Britain, France and Holland, and the subsequent violence, though sometimes directed against foreigners, reflected the division of opinion among Japanese as to the wisdom of opening up the country. This took the form of a civil war in which the sides consolidated around the persons of the Mikado and the Shogun. Even when this was decided in January 1868 by the defeat of the Shogun's forces at Fushimi near Kyoto, and the 'restoration' of the Mikado to full power, the diehards continued to menace all foreigners, making Japan a place where diplomat A.B. Mitford (later Lord Redesdale) said that a foreigner 'carried his life in his hands'.

One of the secrets of the Commodore Perry's success is that he astutely brought on his second visit some specimens and models of western civilisation. For example, a model telegraph, and a steam locomotive and carriage. It was just a model, but the train puffed around a circular track, and the Japanese officials, showing the inherent delight of small boys in steam trains, fell over themselves to take a ride, perched on top of the carriage in their flowing robes, for it was too small for them to get inside.

It is difficult to visualise what Japan was like in the 1860s, when my Grandpa first tasted it as a 26-year-old Assistant Surgeon in the Royal Navy, posted in 1864 to *HMS Euryalis*, of 2,371 tons and 35 guns, flagship of the East Indies & China Squadron. His appointment was 'for duties in *HMS Coromandel*' (a paddle steamer of 303 tons, tender to the flagship). This rather comical posting meant working in the Naval hospital at Yokohama where the Royal Navy had a shore establishment set up under the treaty of 1858. Here he witnessed the arrival in July 1865 of Sir Harry Parkes, our fiery Minister Plenipotentiary in full diplomatic uniform, and they became good friends. Later, Grandpa wrote the biography of Sir Harry, which forms a detailed history of those stormy times. He also witnessed the Shogun's army of 60,000 troops departing from Tokyo 'to bring the unruly Choshu clan to submission. From a hillock overlooking the Tokkaido the present writer watched the curious procession pass by, a strange medley of picturesque medievalism and nineteenth-century westernism', he wrote.

Picture feudal Japan, a mountainous and monsoonal country little bigger than Britain, with no railways, no proper roads, no telegraphs, no postal services, no newspapers; all land transport by horse or human power; all travel for foreigners, when permitted beyond the 20-mile concession area, on horseback, or by *jinrikisha* or *norimon* – heavy enclosed wooden palanquins borne on a beam by four men. When the first telegraph lines went up, peasants used to stare at them, hoping to see the messages going along. When the first post office was opened at Yokohama in 1875, letters were delivered at a run. Nothing strange in that. In Victorian India, dak-runners carried the mails long distances by relays of men. Katie Hickman in her book *Daughters of Britannia: The Lives and Times of Diplomatic Wives* records that the British Consul appointed to Kashgar in Chinese Turkestan received and despatched his mails by dak-runners from Srinagar in Kashmir, a journey across the Himalayas that took 24 days. Relay stations were provided by the Indian government and stocked with provisions and fuel.

Government was in the hands of feudal lords, the Daimyo (from whom the Tokugawa clan provided the Shogun, the temporal ruler), while the Mikado, revered as a divinely appointed ruler, languished impotently in his Kyoto palace. The Daimyo were supported by thousands of armed Samurai who owed them service; the 'two-sworded' men who had the right to slice off the head of anyone who failed to show respect. Then came the peasants, the artisans and last in precedence the merchants. Last of all, and usually ignored in history, the Eta, the outcasts who did the dirty jobs, like Indian Untouchables; and who were not 'liberated' until 1871 – but still suffer prejudice today.

The instability of such a society made for constant danger. Not only did Daimyo war with Daimyo (and all maintained armed forces and sometimes navies), but individuals took it upon themselves to assassinate the foreigners whom they had been taught to despise. Thus the unprovoked murder of a Mr Richardson in 1862, a civilian visitor, caused Colonel Neale, who was Chargé d'Affaires, to demand retribution and compensation from the Shogun. A year's negotiations failing to produce any result, Neale resorted to 'gunboat diplomacy' and despatched the Royal Navy to bombard the fortified town of Kagoshima – which eventually produced results – though the Samurai who wielded the sword was known but escaped punishment.

A year later, the Choshu clan habitually harrassed shipping passing through the Straits of Shimonoseki, the normal route into the Inland Sea leading to Tokyo, Kobe and Osaka. This was contrary to the treaties, and could not be allowed to continue. Rather than acting alone, as at Kagoshima, Sir Rutherford Alcock secured a naval alliance of Britain, France, America and Holland, with a fleet of 17 ships made a thorough job of neutralising the hornet's nest. Two thousand marines were put ashore, the batteries were destroyed and the guns removed. Choshu made peace and agreed to behave in future. With no telegraph nearer than Ceylon, and mail from home taking two months,

Alcock, the man on the spot, had to use his initiative. Sometimes the Foreign Office approved; sometimes not; sometimes as in this case they changed their minds in Alcock's favour.

Another example of violence not involving Samurai, but troops of the Shogun's Army, was the cold-blooded murder of 20 French sailors who were peacefully taking soundings in the Bay of Osaka. Here the Japanese courts ordered the mass execution – by *harikiri* or *seppuku* of 20 men. The French officers witnessing the ceremony were so sickened that after 11 were despatched, they ordered the remainder to be commuted to imprisonment.

A.B. Mitford records in his memoirs that 'in my whole service in Japan I never sat at my desk without a loaded revolver at hand, and never went to bed without a rifle beside me'. With good reason, for he suffered an attack in his bungalow one night by six 'ruffians' who were only repulsed by the joint efforts with swords and guns of himself and his servants. Cleverly, he had spread the surroundings of his bungalow with cockle shells, so that the noise of their approach woke him.

The settlement of Yokohama had British and French garrisons in the 1860s and 1870s, lodged in barracks on the 'Bluff', a hill overlooking the town. Later, in Tokyo, our Legation was provided with a mounted detachment of Metropolitan Police.

By 1865 Grandpa Dickins had been transferred to *HMS Princess Royal*, 3,500 tons and 73 guns, the new flagship, and he was serving in her when the newly arrived Minister, Sir Harry Parkes decided to take her up to visit Hokkaido Island where he was responsible also for the concession of Hakodate. They visited Yurappu, a large village of the Ainu, natives of Hokkaido whose numbers have greatly dwindled. It was here that the friendship started between Dickins and Parkes which was to extend to the end of the century. Dickins writes: 'During the long rides over the hills, along the lake shores, through the birch and pine forests and over the shingly beaches I was often Sir Harry's companion'.

The Treaty Port concessions offered to Britain were Kanagawa (later Yokohama), 18 miles from Tokyo, Nagasaki, and Hakodate in the northern island of Hokkaido. At Yokohama, a small fishing village of about 100 houses, the Shogun's government (known as the Bakufu) hastily built two wharves, a street of shops, and about 20 wooden huts with paper windows for the foreigners. Bounded by the sea, a canal, and a swamp, the settlement was easily turned into an island by two bridges with guardhouses which were closed at night. The intention was to keep the foreigners under close control, as they had done with the Dutch at Nagasaki.

However unsatisfactory Yokohama's site was considered by Sir Rutherford Alcock, our first Minister, it was accepted with alacrity by the commercial fraternity of many nations, who lost no time in building godowns and flooding the wharves with goods for trade. Fortunes were made and lost; in part through the absence of any known method of converting Japanese money into foreign currencies. The Japanese used coins of such miniscule value that the smallest transaction required a sack of cash. Recourse was had mainly to Mexican silver dollars.[1]

Within a very few years, Yokohama became a busy town and port, with western shops, offices, gas-lit streets, hotels and wholesale firms such as Jardine Matheson of Hong Kong fame, whose Director William Keswick took a house there. Initially land was free, but soon houses were bought and sold, and title deeds introduced. A Municipal Council followed, but lasted only two years. Diplomat A.B. Mitford, commenting on the corruption of Japanese customs officials, describes a practice similar to our cross-Channel illegal imports: claiming 'as goods intended for personal use' the import of large quantities of liquor. No wonder we read of every social occasion in those days that 'champagne flowed like water'.

Happy days! Though they sometimes turned bitter, as in Yokohama's great fire of 1866, when a large proportion of houses and godowns, both foreign and native, were reduced to ashes. Mitford lost his entire kit, shortly after arrival. Because of the flimsy wooden houses and paper windows, fire was always Japan's greatest enemy, and firemen were accorded top honours.

The prospects of new markets in trade encouraged a new generation of enterprising expatriates from Britain, Europe and America, who like my Grandpa fell in love with Japan. He grew so fond of the country that he changed his job in order to live there. Resigning from the Navy in 1866, he returned home to qualify as a barrister, and returned in 1871 with a wife to live in Yokohama and practise in the Consular Courts until 1879, raising three children. With so much mayhem and murder, to say nothing of the common emergencies of fire and shipwreck, there must have been plenty of legal work. He prospered, owning and editing a daily and a weekly edition of the *Japan Mail*, and four houses on the bluff.

British Consular Courts were established under a Supreme Court in Shanghai, to which Dickins applied for permission to practise in the concession of Yokohama. Commercial disputes occupied most of the courts' time, and he also appeared in the High Court in Tokyo. One report in the *Japan Mail* has the 'respected barrister F.V. Dickins' arguing with Judge Hannen whether there should be a right of appeal to the Supreme Court in Shanghai. The argument concerned whether a British subject 'carries British law with him wherever he goes, or if he is only subject to law decreed by the Queen in Council'.

---

[1] A Mexican silver dollar costing 4s. 6d. (23p) could be exchanged for a gold token worth 18s. (90p) in any other part of the world (Olive Checkland in *Britains' Encounter with Meiji Japan 1868–1912*).

No wonder Japan found her gold rapidly vanishing; but how could get-rich-quick foreigners be blamed, if the Japanese, through self-imposed ignorance of foreign countries, chose to value their gold so lightly?

In a famous case involving a Chinese coolie who escaped from a Peruvian ship carrying indentured labourers and sought refuge in *HMS Iron Duke*, Dickins used the case as an analogy to attack the system of indentured labour applied to the 'sing-song' girls (i.e. prostitutes) employed in the tea houses of the Yoshiwara, the 'Floating World' romanticised by the woodcut prints of Utamaro, which so enraptured Monet that he filled his house at Giverny with them. As a result of his arguments, an edict was issued 'banning the sale of people to others', which should have put an end to the 'Floating World', but human nature being what it is, within a year the system went on as before. Nevertheless the government did recognise the force of the humanitarian case to the extent of ceasing to draw the dues which were imposed on the documents of indenture. In other words, they washed their hands of it – like Pilate.

Sir Harry Parkes was a remarkable man, irascible and determined, with an iron will under danger. This is typified in a letter to his wife: 'I had an accident the other day. A ruffian cut at me as I was coming home from an interview with the Foreign Minister. Providentially he missed both me and dear old Shah [his dog]. I was going at a rapid pace which interfered with his aim. He had a companion and the street was thronged at the time. It was just getting dusk. I pulled up and turned upon them and succeeded in capturing one – the other dived into a house and got away for the moment, but having secured one of them, the Government were able to learn who the other was, and they captured him the same night. They are now on their trial'.

A far more serious affray had occurred when presenting his credentials in a formal diplomatic visit to the Mikado in Kyoto in March 1868. Sir Harry, with Mitford and Satow as translators, and supported by a guard of honour of the 9th Regiment and a mounted detachment of the Metropolitan Police, and squadrons of Imperial troops fore and aft, rode through the crowded streets to the palace. Unfortunately many fanatical anti-foreigners and supporters of the Shogun were still at large, and the procession was set upon by two desperadoes who ran amok with their deadly swords, slashing wildly at men and horses, killing and wounding several before being overcome. One was beheaded by a Japanese, and the other, wounded, was detained by Mitford, who seems to have acted heroically. Parkes describes to his wife how 'a Japanese rushed past us cutting frantically at everybody as he ran. His blows cleared me, but cut my belt and took off the end of the nose of Satow's pony, which was close to me'.

A year later, one Daimyo still refused to capitulate, and the Admiral of the Tokugawa's fleet, supported by a few French officers, sailed away to Hakodate in Hokkaido and proclaimed a republic – only to be defeated, and the Frenchmen disgraced. The civil war was dragging on in guerilla fashion; yet in the midst of such uncertainties and dangers, the Duke of Edinburgh in 1869 paid a state visit in *HMS Galatea* to the Mikado, in the success of which Mitford again distinguished himself as an organiser.

F.V. Dickins considered it an oversimplification of a very complicated story to speak of the 'Restoration' of the Mikado, henceforth known as the Emperor. Because, he wrote, 'the Mikado never did have the overall power over the whole country, which had been taken away from him and then returned. He was almost always the mere puppet and creature of some clique or party or tribal or clan chiefs, or court nobles, their descendants or military adventurers, the Daimyo or feudal barons of later days'.

Because wealth in Japan was calculated in *koku*, a measure of the quantity of rice which an area could produce, and most of this was in the hands of the Daimyo warlords, there was no store of national wealth to support the currency of the new government of the Emperor. Almost the first thing it did was to apply to the City of London for a loan.

Despite the closed nature of feudal Japan, the ruling class was not entirely ignorant of the western world, and they were acutely aware of their neighbours Korea and China, with which they were periodically at war. The word *kamikaze* describes the 'divine wind' which blew back a Mongol invasion fleet in 1281. Buddhism was received from Korea, and Chinese Confuscianism influenced the native Shinto beliefs.

The Shogun's government, the Bakufu, handled the day-to-day running of the country, and the Mikado, accorded divine origin, was relegated to a figurehead in his Kyoto palace. The Daimyo were really the 'big businessmen'. They could see the Dutch merchants at work in Nagasaki, and there was a trickle of imports. They could see the advantage of steamships for transport of bulk goods such as rice, coal or sugar, and by the 1870s there were many Japanese-owned steamships. International trade was just beginning, but in the absence of efficient land transport, steamers were useful for internal trade. One or two bold spirits broke away to study in the West. The world knows how quickly the Japanese learn, and within a few years they were building roads, railways, steamships, and battleships, mainly with British help, and demonstrating their military might by sinking almost the entire Tsar's fleet at Tsushima in 1905. Only 2 out of 38 Russian ships escaped. The first railway, between Tokyo and Yokohama was opened in 1872 – little more than a hundred years ago.

In feudal Japan, and for some time after its 'opening' clocks were very uncommon, and punctuality unknown in consequence. But having accepted the barbarians, there was intense pressure to catch up with the West, and to adopt its fashions. Satow records a small dance given by the French Admiral, where ladies wore 'short skimping petticoats and high heels in the middle of the feet'. This is hardly an attempt to follow western fashion, but is obviously a description of the *geta*: wooden clogs raising the foot six inches from the ground, with two transverse bars underneath which could perhaps be considered a pair of heels. They are one of the oldest and most traditional of Japanese fashions, still in use by costumed geisha, who clip-clop along on them to a party. Even men are shown on them in old woodcut prints.

49

Another to our eyes really bizarre fashion in vogue among married ladies was to have the teeth blackened and 'polished until they shone like patent leather'. Eyebrows were shaved off and painted in black, high up on the forehead.

For all the beauty of Japan's countryside, its cherry blossom and bonsai pines, its majestic cone of Fuji-san reflected in still waters of a lake bounded by the Torii-gate of a Shinto temple, it is only fair to add the judgement of Mitford who complained that 'the outrageous pride and vanity of the Japanese character passes all belief'. History has proved him right. Can such a character ever change?

Both Mitford (Lord Redesdale) and Satow left memoirs which illuminate in detailed fashion the history of their times in Japan. In Satow's case his life is displayed in a TV film entitled *A Diplomat in Japan*. Filmed in Japan, this conveys the intimate flavour of Japanese life in feudal times, and is so well cast and acted that one feels that these are not actors but the real people. And indeed it is a true story, bringing history alive. It also introduces a touching story of love gained and lost; for both men had Japanese mistresses and produced children, which in the social climate of late Victorianism could not be acknowledged. Marriage to a 'native' would have put paid to diplomatic careers.

Sir Ernest Satow had two sons, and a scene in the film shows him, some years after the happy idyll with his Madame Chrysanthemum was ruptured by an unwelcome posting to Siam, returning for a brief family visit with the boys in their teens, to enjoy a snowbound holiday, which displays some of Japan's most beautiful scenery at Nikko and Lake Chuzenji.

I was prepared to believe that this episode was fictitious, but Olive Checkland gives details of his sons in a footnote in her book *Britain's Encounter with Meiji Japan 1868–1912*. She writes: 'Satow's son Eitaro visited his father in England but because of chest trouble settled in La Sal near Denver in the USA. There he changed his name to Alfred Satow, married Lucy and died in 1926. [In the same year, his father died and was buried at Ottery St Mary in Devon.] 'Ernest Satow is believed to have visited Eitaro at least once. Satow's second son, Hisayoshi (1883–1972) became Dr Takeda, a well-known botanist and a founding member of the Japan Mountain Climbers Association'.

Satow was later promoted to Minister in Japan. He was of an age with my Grandpa Dickins, they studied Japanese together, and remained in correspondence up to Dickins' death in 1915.

As to Mitford, he paid a very short visit to Japan in 1873, and an article in the *Asahi* newspaper in 1985 by Professor Hagihara speculates that this may have been to see his daughter O-Mitsu (a play on Mitford); but she was never mentioned.

Childhood memories of Grandpa's home show that he brought his love of Japan back with him. The house was packed with lacquer cabinets, screens, fans, coloured woodcut prints and suits of Samurai armour of woven bamboo with bulky bewhiskered helmets depicting fierce warriors, designed to strike terror into the enemy. Especially thrilling to an 8-year-old, were two Samurai swords cradled on a red-painted stand, which I was never allowed to touch.

F.V. Dickins was a classical scholar, and among the earliest of translators of Japanese verse. He translated the *Chiushingura, The Story of the 47 Ronin*, known to every Japanese. The Ronin are the 'unemployed' Samurai, deprived of the support of their lords, to whom they still owe allegiance unto death. Still of semi-noble status and armed with their two swords, one long and one short (the latter for use when committing *hara-kiri* or *seppuku*) they were an unhappy class responsible for much of the disorder. And it must be remembered that *seppuku* was an honourable death; to be deprived of it by a common executioner was the ultimate degredation.

Besides volumes of verse totalling over 700 pages in the Library of the Japan Society, Dickins translated two other old folk tales: *The Old Bamboo Hewer's Story*, and *The Magical Carpenter of Japan*. Both are illustrated by woodcut prints of Hokusai, one of the most famous printmakers of the eighteenth and nineteenth centuries. Dickins also published a book with 70 whole-page prints of Hokusai.

The collected works of Dickins were published in 1999 by the Faculty of Oriental Studies of Cambridge University, in seven volumes.

10

Getting to Grips with Japan

Here with a Loaf of Bread beneath the Bough,
a Flask of Wine, a Book of Verse – and Thou
beside me singing in the Wilderness –
And Wilderness is Paradise enow.

The Rubaiyat of Omar Khayyam, Stanza 11

A first visit to Japan is inevitably fraught with excitement and not a little doubt; will you understand this strange country which is seriously different from any other? Particularly if you have seen active service against an enemy noted for its brutality, savagery and cunning; in the three wars which Japan has waged in the modern era, the first blow has always been struck *before* declaration of war. If in addition, you have read all the testimonies of prisoners of Japan: Ronald Searle, Laurens van der Post, 'Weary' Dunlop (the heroic Australian surgeon), Eric Lomas (the 'Railway Man'), you will have a wall of *idées fixes* to overcome before you can even contemplate a visit.

In my case, my Grandpa's experience of falling in love with Japan to such an extent that he changed his job in order to live there, spent half his working life and raised three quarters of his family there, gave me the compelling need to go and see for myself what it was that so attracted him. Not without many qualms, for it was only 25 years since the end of the war, and Japan, though rapidly becoming an 'economic miracle', was by no means fully welcomed back into the comity of civilised nations.

Grandpa had left no family records or diaries to help, but his dedication to Japanese literature proved a boon. I had only to mention that my grandfather had translated into English the *Chiushingura. The Story of the 47 Ronin*, to evoke an 'Ah, so' and a sympathetic interest, for the classic folk tale is known to everyone. Preliminary reading was limited, but one book gave an outline of Japan's history and character of penetrating comprehension. Fosco Maraini's *Meeting with Japan*, in translation from Italian, was published in 1959. Maraini is a noted scholar, mountaineer and linguist, and he lived with his family in Japan before the war. After Italy's surrender in 1943, they were

52

interned, and though as civilians they did not suffer as did POWs, they saw Japan from the inside, at its best and worst.

Maraini is a very fine photographer, and his book is copiously illustrated with his pictures in black and white, with a little colour. As a memoir of travels throughout Japan, and as a history of the country and its religions – the *kami* or spirit which imbues Japanese thinking – Maraini reminds us that 'perhaps no people in the world are more remote from us, more difficult to understand'.

One of the hardest things to remember in modern Japan is that it is only some 150 years since the black ships of American Commodore Perry forced the closed country to open its shores to the West. Hitherto the sole contact had been the trading post, first Portuguese, then Dutch on artificial Deshima island, in Nagasaki harbour. Japan knew nothing of railways, telephones, and had no international commerce, which was swirling all around her, penetrating from the growing trade of China via the increasing number of foreign Concessions along its coast. In Japan it was not until 1858 that the first Concessions were negotiated at Yokohama, Nagasaki and Hakodate, for the British, French, Dutch and Americans. Almost immediately, many foreign firms were established, including Jardine Matheson, famous for their part in China's opium trade.

Japan seems never to have acquired the taste for opium. Almost her only wholesale trade was in rice and coal, which had to be moved in bulk, and this was so expensive without any means of bulk carriage, that Japanese entrepreneurs lost no time in acquiring foreign ships for transport by sea. But it was still internal trade. The speed with which western urbanisation developed is indicated in *A Diplomat's Wife in Japan*, the recollections of Mary Crawford Fraser, which has one of those coloured wood block prints depicting a broad street in the Ginza district of Tokyo in 1884. It shows rows of two-storey modern shops, some higher buildings, street lighting, two horse-drawn trams, an open carriage, a delivery van, and figures in Victorian dress.

Modern Japanese mega-cities are as ugly as any in the world. As elsewhere, tree-lined streets of gracious houses set in their own gardens are dwarfed by massive concrete blocks, towering skyscrapers and soulless motorways. The question for the first-time visitor is, will you find anything of the old, romantic, spiritual Japan of cherry blossom, moon-gazing parties, cormorant fishing, topless women pearl divers, archery and sumo contests, mystical incense-filled Zen temples and vast processions of costumed crowds bearing huge archaic chariots? The answer is yes and no; it depends if you have your eyes open; if you see with the third eye of Buddha.

In Tokyo your taxi driver will wear a uniform and white gloves, and will bow to you. He will not expect a tip, and it would be bad form to offer him one, suggesting that he is badly paid. You will probably be staying in the New Otani Hotel, a favourite with package tours, a 40-storey tower with a Japanese garden of ten acres below.

Relief at finding they drive on the left will rapidly evaporate at the sight of the streams of traffic squeezed into the narrowest of streets. It is like the human body; arterial blood squeezed under pressure through veins and capillaries. Attempts to relieve the pressure by elevated expressways, flyovers and tunnels are limited by sheer lack of space between buildings, which have been constructed far too close together – just like London.

However, it is when you leave the modernised centres of the cities and wander through the alleyways of Nara or Kyoto (former capitals) that you find out why the Japanese are so clever at miniaturisation. The houses are all tiny to start with, and if you look down from a height, anywhere in the country, on an ocean of multi-coloured tile roofs, it is like a model village. The streets, seldom more than single lane, are still further restricted by the electric cables being all external, supported on poles, making the street an obstacle course. If you think we are overcrowded, try the subway at rush hour. When I visited the home of a quite senior official, the sitting room of his two-room flat was about the size of two first-class railway compartments; a table in the middle, and seats down each side. Computers and TV took up the rest of the space.

A population of 126 million, in a country only 25 per cent larger than the British Isles, would not necessarily mean serious overcrowding. But what tips the scale is the fact that 75 per cent of Japan's area is mountainous and forested, incapable of being developed either for housing or for paddy fields. That is what makes the country so beautiful, but it may partly explain Japan's historic urge to aggressively expand.

In few countries is the contrast between ancient and modern more extreme than in Japan, where cities like Tokyo, Osaka, Nagoya or Kobe, with their skyscrapers, huge department stores, hotels and underground railway contrast with straggling royal palaces, Buddhist and Shinto temples of every variety, and beautifully landscaped gardens. Although apparently old, these buildings are not necessarily so, because the delicate structures of wood, and the paper-covered sliding doors and windows have made them so combustible that there are few traditional buildings that have not been rebuilt several times. The Shinto Shrines of Ise, dedicated to the sun goddess Amaterasu, the founder of the nation, are rebuilt by tradition every 20 years. Only the castles, lairs of feudal Daimyo with the power of life and death over their former subjects, have an impressive bulk, rising like pyramids of many-storeyed towers, built upon a foundation of huge stones. They compare as symbols of absolute territorial power with the forbidding menace of our medieval castles. In Tokyo, where guided tours of the grounds of the post-war concrete Imperial Palace take place with special permission, this lone *gaikokujin* joined what appeared to be an afternoon stroll of a Mothers' Union Branch; plump mama-sans shepherded by a smart uniformed official. Stepping out of line to photograph the Emperor's Music Pavilion – an attractive modern piece of architecture – caused no end of consternation. Such indiscipline!

Kyoto is the magnet that draws most visitors to Japan, but Nikko is a site much nearer to Tokyo, in fact just a short train ride away, which demonstrates the finest example of seventeenth-century art in Japan. This is Toshogu Shrine, the mausoleum of Ieyasu Tokugawa, who founded the Shogunate. Approached via an avenue of tall stately cryptomerias, the Japanese cedar, the shrine is a complex of buildings, brilliantly coloured and decorated with symbolic figures; even the 'Three Wise Monkeys' are included. Dating from 1634 to 1636, Nikko is a statement of the Tokugawa confidence in power, which indeed lasted until their overthrow by the Meiji imperial line in 1868. Toshogu is a Shinto shrine, entered under the traditional *torii*, (arch) but Shintoism and Buddhism are closely allied; some later Shoguns were Buddhists. It is often said that most Japanese enter the world as Shintoists, but leave it as Buddhists.

Reverting to Kyoto, its 'sights' are perhaps so well known that further description is superfluous, but it is worth remembering that while it is one of the Imperial capitals, it has both an Imperial Palace, traditional home of the Mikado, and a palace where the Shogun lived when visiting the Emperor which all Daimyo were required to do annually, to establish their nominal fealty. Hence all the travelling on the Tokaido road by nobles and their retainers, so well depicted by Hiroshige in his prints '53 Stages of the Tokaido Highway'.

When returning to their fiefdoms, the clans were required to leave behind one member of their family as a hostage; there wasn't any love lost between them, and nobody trusted anything but power. The Shogun's Nijo Castle is not really a castle, but a series of low-ceilinged corridors and halls leading to the throne room, decorated with superb wall paintings of storks, tortoises, contorted pine trees in green, indigo and black on a golden background; original work of Naonobu Kano of the seventeenth century. The 'Nightingale Floors' were designed to squeak when trodden on, to give warning of approaching danger.

Naturally there is a garden, exquisitely landscaped around a pond, but this doesn't compare with the gardens of the Imperial Palace, which cover 27 acres, and are surrounded by the Imperial Park which covers 220 acres. Quite a big green belt for royalty, but it was formerly used also for the imperial princes and high court nobles. Some distance away on the Katsura river is the Katsura Imperial Villa, a summerhouse set among lakes, bridges, tea-houses, waterfalls, stone lanterns, a countryside created by specially selected rocks; all the features which make up a Japanese garden, which does *not* include formal flower beds. Permission is needed for a visit, which provided me with features on Japanese Gardens for *Country Life* and *Homes and Gardens*.

Almost a trade mark of Kyoto is the Golden Pavilion set in a lake at Kinka-kuji temple, built by a retiring Shogun in 1397, for meditation. Twice burnt down, it was last rebuilt in 1955. Equally popular is Ryoanji temple, the best known example of a Zen rock garden; nothing but fifteen rocks in a bed of sand enclosed by a low stone wall. A companion to this is Ginkakuji, known as the Silver Pavilion, with a sand garden representing Mount Fuji. My favourite is Tofukuji temple, which includes many sub-temples with gardens of sand, rocks, moss and pines, besides a very handsome large building with high-ridged eaves. Also Kiyomizu, high above the city on the valley slopes. (8th century).

Kyoto is supreme, but one cannot ignore Nara, which boasts both the oldest wooden building in the world, the five-storeyed pagoda at Horyuji temple; but also the largest statue of Buddha, the Daibutsu, at Todaiji temple, which is also the largest wooden building in the world. The bronze Buddha weighs 452 tons, and was cast (on site, naturally) over four years from 745 to 749. A record that is unlikely to be achieved today. It is far, far bigger than the giant Buddha at Kamakura. Nara was the capital for most of the 8th century.

No visit to Japan should omit a night or two in a Ryokan, an Inn where everything is done in the traditional style. The privacy and personal attention are highly agreeable, and minister to one's self-esteem. Even a clumsy *gaiko-kujin* (foreigner) is unlikely to be unaware of the necessity of removing outdoor shoes before entering a Japanese private house. In any event, he will be relieved of his at the door of a Ryokan and given a pair of slippers – which will probably be too small. Arrived in his room, his problems are not over. The house slippers should be exchanged for another category, the room slippers; and even this is not the end, for when he shuffles down the corridor to the O-Furo (the bathroom) he will be expected to put on a special *benjo* (toilet) slipper. He will be provided with a Yukata, a cotton bathrobe, which is the normal wear in the room, and will serve very well as pyjamas. The room will be furnished with a low lacquer table, where you sit on the floor for your meals with feet underneath. Knowing how uncomfortable for foreigners this position is, most Ryokans will provide a backrest which gives slight support. There will be a *tokonoma* or decorative panel, against which the senior member of the party should sit, with an *ikebana* of perhaps a single flower. Very likely, as at my first Ryokan, a window or doorway will overlook a tiny private garden, a raked path, a clipped azalea, a small pond.

On my first visit, I was not well briefed on bathing etiquette. I did not expect to share a bath with a beautiful girl or anything like that, as so often shown in films, but I did not understand the principle of soaping and washing first, then soaking in the bath. Confronted with a square wooden tub about 3 feet high, brimming with scalding water, it was impossible to consider getting into it until letting out half and adding cold water. Having bathed as I would at home, I discovered I had forgotten to bring a towel, so with yukata covering my wet and lobster-pink body, I tiptoed back to my room.

The Yukata and slippers and often a toothbrush as well, are supplied as routine in all Japanese hotels, which explains why it is possible to travel with practically no luggage. My guides never carried even a small suitcase; just a cotton bag no larger than a lady's purse. My guides, who often lived well outside Tokyo and had to get up at an ungodly hour in order to put me on a morning train as early as 0700 or 0800, were a pretty good lot on the whole. But there are exceptions to all good things, and I cannot resist a verbatim quote from my diary on one unfortunate young man.

'F really gets in my hair; so vulgar and completely insensitive. Drops ash everywhere, sits down on a book or paper without noticing it, flooded the train floor with beer, and sat us in the wrong seats. Hair like a birdsnest, always smoking and eating, which he describes as his main job. Jabbles incessantly in barely coherent English, and never listens to what is said to him. He ate some ghastly concoction of cuttle fish and his breath stank the compartment out. Made him travel with window open, despite a cold wind.'

Never mind! We had dinner together next day, cooked in my room Ryokan-style, though in a modern hotel. After some days on the west coast, off the tourist beaten track, a three and a half hour train journey through alpine scenery of gorges, tunnels and forests, brought us to Kurashiki, a beauty spot laced with canals, bridges, graceful trees, and low white houses with wooden grill windows, over a century old. Schoolchildren, all in uniform, were apparently on holiday, and a couple of model girls were being posed with cars above the canals. They were surprised to be shot by a gaiko-kujin photographer too.

Of my four visits to Japan, one was in a small press trip; the others were as a guest of the Japan National Tourist Organisation and Japan Airlines, for whose help I am very grateful. I have often travelled in foreign countries without any common language; but when one wants to pursue a serious study of its history and arts, it is better that one's footsteps be guided, and questions answered through a native.

I was shown not only the regular tourist sights, but also many offbeat places like Mizushima, a vast industrial complex built on reclaimed land, a tribute to modern planning, but where pollution from all the factories and oil refineries has destroyed every fish in the bay. We took in the Ise Shima National park, Ago Bay where I photographed the women pearl divers and the rafts of maturing oysters; and over the Japanese Alps to fishing villages on the Japan Sea, to Kurashiki and Matsue. It was at Matsue that Lafcadio Hearn, the Greek–Irish Americanised teacher and journalist settled. He became naturalised and married a Japanese girl, and poured out a series of books extolling his love of Japan. The similarity to my Grandpa's story intrigued me; though Hearn came later, in the 1880s and he died in 1904, the year before the Japanese Navy sank the Tsar of Russia's fleet at Tsushima. Even so, when Hearn travelled from Yokohama to Matsue to take up his appointment as Professor of English, it was a four day journey by jinrickisha over the mountains.

Lafcadio Hearn's stories bear witness to the stamina and hardiness of the jinrickisha runners, who would persevere tirelessly for many hours, heads sheltered from rain by rush jackets. A temperament with which we were made all too familiar in the war. I had cause to remember the 'little yellow men' as we thought of them then, pushing their bikes through the rubber plantations of the Malaysian jungle, as they descended on Singapore, carrying their rations in a bag of rice.

So Grandpa must have travelled by *jinrickisha* too; or possibly in a *norimon* a palanquin, a three foot square box, slung on a pole between four bearers, more suited to a brace of chickens or a pig going to market. Horses were available of course, and for recreation Grandpa used to go riding with Sir Harry Parkes, Britain's Minister to Japan, with whom he was friendly and wrote his biography, which is one of the histories of the Meiji Restoration. Since the opening of the Treaty Ports, there were always plenty of ships around; mail steamers, naval ships from little paddle boats and gunboats to modern cruisers, and the Admiral's yacht. These provided many excursions not available to inland transport, and Grandpa took part in one to the northern island of Hokkaido, where some of the indigenous Ainu remained.

Matsue is one of the most traditional Japanese provincial towns, dominated by its great castle, a medieval monster of the same general type as that of Osaka, on which the story and the film of James Clavell's *Shogun* is based. It is typical of the feudal fortresses of the Daimyo who wielded the power and of whom the Shogun was the chief, and with whom the foreign powers had originally to deal because the Emperor, the ruler-in-name, of Divine origin was relegated to a figurehead, in his Kyoto palace.

Matsue was the home of Kyutaro Moriyama, a noted 'Tea Master'; that is a teacher of the tea ceremony (Cha-no-yu) which was introduced in Zen Buddhist monasteries in the 15th century, though green tea had been drunk since the 8th century. It became more and more stereotyped and teachers of the etiquette acquired aesthetic fame. The essence of it is simplicity of design and ornament, the bowls being of the roughest stoneware, the room tiny, with a low door through which one must crawl to enter, imposing humility, decoration limited to a lacquer table, and the *tokonoma* or porch with a simple *Ikebana* arrangement of flowers or branches. Understatement is of the essence, but when it comes to the prescribed movements of making and serving the tea, then precision is required; every last detail is prescribed and taught. Tedious it may sound, but calming it is. All this Moriyama taught me and demonstrated; but I found that many of the demonstrations put on for the benefit of tourists are mechanical and fall short of the spirit. Indeed, there is evidence that the whole mystique has been prostituted by commercial promotion; expensive schools of training and high-priced public shows which become a marque of fashion.

11

In Father's Footsteps

Oh East is East and West is West
And never the Twain shall meet,
Till Earth and Sky stand presently
at God's great Judgment Seat;
But there is neither East nor West,
Border nor Breed, nor Birth,
when two strong men stand face
to face, tho' they come from the
ends of the Earth.

Kipling

Note: Most people are familiar with only the first two lines, and condemn the poem as racist. This misses the point entirely, which is that before God there is no such thing as 'racism'.

As a link between two centuries and three generations, my father stood in the middle, betwixt Grandpa and I. His entirely Asiatic career of 36 years was followed by 40 years of retirement. Joining the Royal Garrison Artillery in the last year of the Boer War, and witnessing the funeral of Queen Victoria, his career was as typical as any could be of an age which has passed.

Duty was the key which took him from service in Ceylon, to Hong Kong, Burma, India, Aden, and to a little over a year in France during the Great War, when the Second Indian Cavalry Division was sent to 'reinforce' the trench warfare. By 1916, he (but not the horses) was sent back to India as 'reinforcement' for a suspected German plot to invade India.

Father left an unpublished memoir which records some interesting statistics. Over a period of 24 years, he had 22 postings. Though a married officer since 1906, he never acquired a house or furniture until after retirement. In India, furniture was always hired, despite (or because of) the frequent postings. With seven journeys home, that involved 29 complete packing and unpacking of all worldly goods. Then there were nine trips to hill stations – not including the final seven years as a senior officer in delectable Simla, in a hotel. Quite a gypsy-like existence. But quite typical.

Naturally I followed in his footsteps in practically all the places he knew, and thousands that he didn't. For his first posting. Trincomali, he arrived by the Orient liner *Orizaba* (only 5,000 or 6,000 tons) at Colombo, then after a few days sightseeing to Mount Lavinia and Kandy went by a small steamer which plied regularly around the island to Trincomali harbour, which he described as: 'a vast land-locked sheet of water, surrounded by dense jungle and low green hills, capable of holding the whole of the then very large British navy – beautiful to look at, but full of sharks'.

Fort Frederick, where a handful of officers controlled a garrison recruited mainly from southern Ireland ('magnificent specimens of humanity, but a pretty tough lot to control'), was built by the Dutch in 1675. The fort was on a headland falling 300 feet sheer into the sea, and as I toured the grassy ramparts, old barrack blocks now converted into offices, and the cemetery where some hundreds of gravestones included both British and Dutch, it seemed a romantic but lonely spot. Across the harbour, where the Navy had its headquarters, life was easier, and the Admiral had a magnificent house. The cause of malaria had only recently been discovered in 1901, and the RAMC Doctor kept a few specimens of the anopheles mosquito in a bottle to identify them.

Service life involves many hardships, but it also grants the occasional unexpected bonus, and father's lucky break came when his Company (the RGA have Companies, not Batteries like other artillerymen) was transferred to Hong Kong. Instead of going by some small and cramped troopship or liner, he was given passage aboard the latest 11,000-ton cruiser, *HMS Amphi-trite*★, and enjoyed both Christmas and Hogmanay aboard, with naval hospitality.

Hong Kong, whose harbour again 'could contain the whole of the largest navy' must have been close to paradise for a young man, something like as depicted in that splendid film *Love is a Many-Splendoured Thing*. The duties of a junior Subaltern were not arduous; the technicalities of cannon fire, range, velocity of shot, care of ammunition; and ceremonial duties for which full dress was in 'whites'. The Peak Tram was already operating, and the Royal Artillery mess of about 20 officers was beside a mid-station. The mess included the future Lord Dowding, who even then was known as 'Stuffy'.

To quote father on life in Hong Kong: ' "Stonecutters" Island and Lyemun Pass (the narrows at the northern end of the harbour) were strongly fortified, and in both places I have spent a month at a time in charge of the detachment of gunners manning the forts; rather a lonely job, but I enjoyed it. What I did not enjoy was having to turn out an Indian Infantry guard on top of a hill, after midnight. The road passed through innumerable Chinese graves,

---

★Built in 1896 by Vickers at Barrow. She could do 20¾ knots, had four funnels and 30 boilers. Her armament was 16 6-inch quick-firing, 14 12-pounders, also QF, and sundry smaller guns.

consisting of bones placed inside earthenware jars, frequently broken and the bones scattered about. I did not like the sight of human skulls grinning at me in the moonlight, and walked very quickly indeed'.

At this point I must interpose my shared experience with father, as Duty Officer at RAF Station Vizagapatam in 1943 when at 10.30 p.m. a driver with a 15cwt truck would rouse me from a mellow evening in the mess, to inspect airfield security, passing from our village of thatched huts, through palms and scrub, to ensure the guards were awake. But Vizag was such a peaceful place, there was nothing to scare one but a barking dog, and moonlight often gave it a romantic touch.

A frequent diversion from Hong Kong was to take a steamer up the Pearl River to Canton, and father describes a 'beam' steamer which must have been unique, even for 1903: 'It was a paddle boat, and the paddle wheels were driven by an engine which moved one end of a beam pivoted in the centre, while the other end was attached to a jointed rod which drove the paddle wheels. The beam protruded well above the deck, and it was a fascinating sight to see it solemnly moving up and down'.

Again, he travelled in a stern-wheeler, the British Captain of which was subsequently murdered, and his body thrown in the river. They would stay a few days in a hotel on the Shameen, the area allotted to the 'factories' of the European traders before and during the Opium Wars of the 1840s. They would take a rickshaw to the White Cloud Mountains, then as now a beauty spot for picnics at a monastery.

Picturesque old Canton may have been, with its thousands of sampans on which whole families were born, lived and died; and the larger sea-going junks with their matting sails, carved high poops so reminiscent of medieval ships; but you needed a strong stomach among the low stone shops in streets barely a yard wide, filled with exotic produce and signs, and Chinamen all wearing pigtails.

Father again: 'Once a friend and myself, walking down the Potters' Lane, found ourselves passing a pile of freshly severed heads on one side, and a sprawling mass of dead bodies on the other – perhaps 30 or 40, we did *not* stay to count. We were told they had been a group of pirates who had been convicted that morning. Pirates were very active in the China seas, and on the steamers plying between Hong Kong and Canton the lower-class Chinese were herded behind iron bars, and armed police guards set over them. There were several cases of Chinese crews murdering their European officers and seizing the ship and its cargo. The British navy had the job of trying to smoke out the pirates'.

He continues: 'A brother subaltern attended a Magistrate's Yamen to watch a trial. When one of the witnesses would not give the required evidence, he had his wrists and ankles broken by blows with a bar. In another case, an Attaché friend of mine in Peking had the nerve to watch the execution of an old woman, for the murder of her husband, by 'Ling Chi' or the death of a thousand cuts. She was tied to a wooden cross, and bit by bit the flesh was cut off her'.

From Hong Kong in 1903, with a brother subaltern, father made 'perhaps the most interesting trip I have ever made. First we sailed to Shanghai, which struck me as rather an American-looking city, with tall, fine buildings, a lot of traffic, obviously a very prosperous commercial town. On Bubbling Wells Road the substantial houses of the tycoons stood in green gardens, and in the club was the longest bar in the world. We stayed two or three days, then took a ship of the Russian Volunteer Fleet to Dairen in Manchuria. (On the point of the peninsula which projects from the north-east into the great Bay of Tientsin.) These ships were very comfortable and fast for these days. In reality they were intended to become commerce-destroyers in wartime. It was the first ship I had travelled in with brass bedsteads instead of the usual bunks. The food was excellent and vodka was provided, like water, in glass jugs on the table. The Captain and officers kept themselves completely remote from the passengers.

'This part of Manchuria had virtually been taken over by the Russians, much to the disgust of the Chinese, and a branch line of the great Trans-Siberian Railway had been built down to Dairen. [Dalny as it then was.] We travelled a short distance by luxurious train and crossed a river to Newchwang [now Yinkow] where the British were established, and then travelled on the British-built railway to Shan-hai-kwan [now Linyu] where the Great Wall comes down to the sea. The train was primitive. Our first-class carriage resembled the French '8 *chevaux* 40 *hommes*' which we knew in the World War. It contained just a wooden table and four wooden chairs. In this luxury we trundled along through a country which was completely sandy desert, for six or seven hours. For a long stretch, there shimmered away to the west a remarkable mirage of lakes, mountains and trees. What could it have been?

'At Linyu was stationed an Indian Army Battalion, aftermath of the Boxer Rising, at whose mess we had a meal, then went on by rail to Peking, with a night stop at Tientsin. Here I cashed a cheque at the Hong Kong & Shanghai Bank, the manager of which was totally blind – surely a unique case.[1]

'In Peking, the hotel where we stayed was, so far a I know, the only one, and like the railway station, was outside the immense walls. Like the Forbidden City, there was little we could see in Peking. I remember the Temple of Heaven, but it was in a terrible state of dirt and neglect. The Lama Temple left an impression of peace and solemnity, with vast black and red curtains, priests moving silently about, in an atmosphere of incense. The

---

[1]The HSBC confirms in 1999 that the manager of their Tientsin Branch in 1903 was a Mr D.H. Mackintosh, but have no evidence that he was blind. They suggest that perhaps my father was the subject of a small leg-pull.

inscription LEST WE FORGET was incised in the stone lintel of the door of the rebuilt wall of the British Legation.

'From Peking we made a short excursion on mule back, with a mule cart containing our guide and our provisions for two or three days, to visit the Great Wall at the Nakau Pass. I remember more vividly the night we spent in a fortified town on one of the hills. We clattered through the gateway in its crenellated walls, into a typical Chinese huddled town. While waiting for our dinner, we watched the armed sentry shoulder his halberd – a real, old-world halberd – as he gave a great shout as the massive gates shut with a clang at nightfall, and the watch-fires were kindled and flickered into the sky, and shone on the little collection of people in front of the gate, and on the ring of low houses round the open space. It was as if one had been transplanted to another, and a slightly theatrical world and time. Here were we two, the only Europeans, placed among people, not only of another race, but apparently of another world and century. Never have I ever again been so conscious of the difference between *us* and *them*.

'At Peking we joined forces with two very pleasant American cavalry officers, who were, rather strange to say, on their way to Oxford University. We embarked at Taku on a Japanese ship with a Norwegian Captain. I remember the date on the ship's bell (1879) because it was the year of my birth. In those days Japanese liners were, I think, always foreign built, and generally captained by Europeans. But they were starting to build their own ships, as opposed to junks, and in Hong Kong harbour we saw the first battle-ship built in Japan: the *Mikasa**, a black, evil-looking thing. The crew were, of course, all Japanese, and even a landlubber like myself could see how quick, smart, and efficient they were. It was the British Navy on which the Japanese fashioned themselves, down to the uniform.

'We put in at Chemulpo [now Inchon], the Korean port connected by a Japanese-built railway with the capital, Seoul; and an extremely comfortable train it was. The Japanese were even then infiltrating deeply into Korea, which they annexed seven years later, in 1910, and ruled until their defeat in 1945. We spent 48 hours in Seoul, in green, hilly country, full of paddy fields. In a large modern theatre we watched a puppet play, very well done, but whose plot we naturally could not follow. However there were one or two incidents for which the term indecent would hardly be adequate. I remember the quaint hats worn by the men, like those tall, stovepipe black hats that Welsh women used to wear.

---

*Father was misinformed. The *Mikasa* was built by Armstrong at Elswick, launched in 1900, of 15,140 tons displacement, with 4 12-inch guns and 14 6-inch. She was Admiral Togo's flagship at the battle of Tsushima: was sunk in 1905 by a magazine explosion, but was recovered and re-armed, and is now preserved in concrete as a national monument at Yokosuka, together with the opposing battleship *USS Midway*.

'We sailed round the south end of Korea to Pusan, and thence to Nagasaki in Japan. A short train trip brought us to a beauty spot nearby, where after lunch at a delightful inn, I fancied having a hot bath. I was ushered to a huge tub, at least four feet high, with a smiling and very pretty Japanese girl waiting beside it with soap, sponge and towel. The tub was only a few feet away from the drive leading to the hotel entrance. Seeing that there was no escape, and that none of the passers-by took the slightest notice, I stripped and allowed myself to be washed, sponged and dried by the girl. The water was extremely hot. My companion was too cowardly to undergo the same treatment.

'From Nagasaki we went to a health resort which treated with mud baths. This was at the foot of an active volcano, Mount Asama, up the slopes of which we were carried in chairs. If you poked your stick into the ground, a little jet of steam puffed up. And so, from Nagasaki, back to Hong Kong, with memories of a world now vanished.'

Picking up the thread of my plot, Darjeeling seems to have played quite a large part, for it enters into the narrative from infancy to age.

Reel 4

Glimpses from the Amphitheatre of Asia

12

Darjeeling in Youth and Age

The cure for this ill is not to sit still,
or frowst with a book by the fire;
But to take a large hoe and a shovel also,
and dig till you gently perspire.
           'How the Camel Got His Hump', Kipling's *Just So Stories*

Darjeeling, queen of the hill stations, and source of India's finest tea. unexcelled for Himalayan views, when dawn tints the five peaks of Kanchenjunga, it is a cherished memory for any visitor. Mine go back rather further than most, and total at a rough calculation seven or eight, starting at age 2, when family annals record that I almost died from bronchitis. My temperature would not go down, until the doctor, in despair, counselled taking all my clothes off and holding me out of the window until I cooled down. It worked, and ever since cold has never troubled me, only heat.

Adding up two wartime leave visits, each involving a 48-hour train journey from southern India, three visits in recent years, and probably three during childhood, it is no wonder that memories are clear, even extending to the locally-engaged Tibetan *ayah*, and the 'dooley' or carrying chair for children, escorted by two bearers. And getting off the miniature train at watering stops during the five-hour ascent, to pick wild flowers in the jungle alongside the track. The earliest journeys would have been more complicated than today, for they involved a break in the railway line on the plains, for a crossing of the Ganges by a ferry – later bridged.

Once during the war, I was sent up on sick leave following a bout of dengue fever and lodged in the Army Hospital at Lebong (the smallest racecourse in the world). A compulsory salt- and fat-free diet was so disgusting that after two days I discharged myself and resumed the fleshpots.

Leave was a sore expense to young Army officers in Edwardian days, and we did not always go to Darjeeling. Once we went to Kurseong which is slightly lower and cheaper than Darjeeling, and also there were seaside holidays at Puri on the Bay of Bengal, where I remember the beach being so flat that you could

67

wade out for miles without going above your knees. It was always a mystery how an impecunious young Subaltern stationed in the semi-underground Fort William on the banks of the River Hoogly in Calcutta could support a wife and child, and of course the retinue of servants required. But manage they did, and by about 1912, now in a big two-storey bungalow at Dum Dum, with lawns and a garden bordered by jungle where jackals howled at night, father actually ran a car! It was a 1909 single cylinder Darracq. After a series of mishaps, including being hauled out of a ditch by a bullock cart, the expenses defeated him, and the car was left with a garage in settlement of repair costs. Dum Dum, of course, is now the site of Calcutta's airport.

Besides an *ayah* to look after me, of whom I saw far more than mother, we had a series of British nursemaids; obviously not a great success, judging from their rapidly changing succession. The one who came out with us when I was 6 months old disappeared one fine day, and was tracked down by the police to a hotel on Chowringhee (the Piccadilly of Calcutta), where she was installed with a Drum Sergeant Major of the Gordon Highlanders.

When Mother brought me home in 1914, partly because my younger brother was due later that year, some idiot of a doctor (an Englishman) had pronounced me as anaemic with a 'murmur' in the heart. The doctors at home fell for this, and treated it with a remedy which still makes me feel sick when I think of it. Take seven pounds of ox liver, they prescribed, and hang it in the larder to drip blood. When a pint has accumulated, make the child drink it. Ugh! That is a true story which turns doctors today pink with shame.

Normally Mother would have returned to India with my brother, leaving me with Granny Mackay, but fate intervened in the shape of the First World War. It was impossible to secure civilian passages, so we three were stranded in Blighty for the duration. One consequence was that I scarcely knew my Father for the rest of childhood and all adolescence: all that I saw of him was on occasional home leaves. That was the common fate of those serving in the Empire (expatriates we call them today); and it is not without its malevolent influence on a child's development – for which I make no excuses for any defects in my character. It was simply the way the cards fell: we didn't hold psycho-babble inquests in those days. Granny was a Victorian rock during adolescence after the war; but being widowed, we lived in a hotel. That was scarcely a 'home'.

How different it is today, when expatriate children can be flown home for school and back for the hols – if you are wealthy enough, or in the Diplomatic Service.

On my first return to Darjeeling after the second war, in 1969, there were some changes. Cars were allowed, where previously only the Viceroy and the Governor of Bengal could drive. Rickshaws had disappeared; just as well, for the heavy coach-built Victorian ones required four pullers to cope with the steep hills on which Darjeeling is dispersed. There had been a serious landslip six months before, destroying large sections of rail and road, so it was a road journey this time, 56 miles from Badogra, the rail and air terminus. Trains were running with shuttle service, either side of the break, and it was good to see the same old Glasgow-built engines of two-foot gauge, dated 1913, that had been running in the war. In the landslip, several coaches of a train were swept down the *khud* (mountain slope), but the guard was so alert that he got all the passengers out in time. Some houses were swept away with sleeping occupants.

In 1969, the Himalayan Mountaineering Institute, of which Sherpa Tensing Norkey was a prominent member, was very active, and I found him busy training some students on rocky slopes, producing future Sherpa climbing guides. He was 55 but looked 40; knew he was a celebrity, but remained simple in manner.

On Observatory Hill, where there is a joint Hindu-Buddhist shrine, priests of both religions were officiating to celebrate the tenth anniversary of the Revolt of the Women in Lhasa, and crowds assembled to hoist the Tibetan flag, after which tea was served. There are some quite wealthy Tibetans (as well as very poor) in Darjeeling, having brought out gold and jewels, and built houses, and a new monastery where I met the Karmapa. There are several other Tibetan monasteries, including a famous one at Ghoom, the summit of the railway line, at 7,400ft.

Higher than that, at Jalapahar, is the military depot, and higher still, at Katapahar, the Gurkha Recruiting Depot at about 8,000ft. I climbed up, hoping to interview the Adjutant, but was rudely pushed away by Indian sentries (not Gurkhas). All India was touchy because of the reverse their army had suffered from a Chinese invasion on the border in 1962.

The club, formerly Planters Club, was managed by an English lady, ex-Kenya and Nepal, who had a black labrador and a tiny bulbul which she had rescued and reared when it fell out of the nest in Kenya. It was completely tame, and perched on my hand and head. Talking to the barman, he bemoaned the rocketing price of rice. Before the war, he said, his wages were only Rs.17 to 20 a month; but enough rice for him and his family cost only Rs.5. I heard the same story elsewhere. If a man had a tiny patch of land to grow vegetables, he could live on Rs.5 a month. For landless peasants, of course, it was a different matter. Another thing the barman regretted was the departure of the Sahibs and Memsahibs, who employed seven servants, and thus supported 20 or more people. Now, he said, the brown Sahibs employ only one.

It took me back to my 1943 Darjeeling leave, which corresponded with the victory of our armies in Tunisia. This conclusion of the Desert War brought great joy and a great *tamasha* (celebration), for India's volunteer armies shared in our pride. A volunteer army of two and a half million is the greatest the world has ever seen. The streets of Darjeeling were full of Union flags and cheering people, as parades of soldiers, Gurkha police, and even monks from one of the Tibetan monasteries, marched through the steep streets to the central Chowrasta.

Government House, where the government of Bengal transfers for the hot weather, was opened for a dance, which at first was proposed to be for officers only, but that idea was quickly ridiculed, and as Darjeeling was chock full of all ranks on leave the crush was tremendous and continued until we staggered home by moonlight.

Switching fast-forward from 1943 to 1969 and 1971, we find India in trouble again, with Pakistan east and west, and with China. Bangladeshi guerillas are making progress against Pakistan's army in their demand for independence, and China is still threatening Himalayan borders. America is sending U2 spy planes over China, and dropping listening devices in the remote Himalayas. SNAFU.

One more time, 1983, and its by road again, because the train is so slow, five and a half hours for 56 miles, and so dirty. (Murray's *Guide* 1965 advises: 'Spectacles or veils should be worn against the dust and blacks from the engine, especially on the front seats of the open carriages from which the best views are obtained'.) We stopped at Sukna where the low tea grows, and crowds overflowed the rails for a bazaar, where a pig was being cut up and sold in pieces wrapped in banana leaves. Rain came on, turning the road into a river. Above Kurseong there was a heavy snowfall, leaving about six inches on the road. A truck had gone off the road, straight down the almost vertical *khud*, and an Army recovery vehicle was having problems wiring it up. But they were sappers, and would cope. The little railway never ceases to amaze, looping the loop, and in the steepest sections zig-zagging backwards and forwards like a schooner tacking, but with prodigious puffing and wheel-slipping, mitigated by the two men who ride on the buffers, throwing sand on the line for better grip. (British Rail never tried *that* when they experienced 'the wrong kind of snow'). Since the train follows the road for much of the way, you have a good view when driving.

The best of India's schools are run on English Public School lines, or sometimes by religious orders, and originally of course with English teachers. Few of these remain, but Anglo-Indians have often taken their places. The Bishop Cotton School at Simla is a good example. The Princes' school at Ajmer, set up in Victorian days exclusively for the Rajkumaris, sprigs of Maharajahs, is another. At Darjeeling is a surfeit of schools. The Loreto Convent for girls, St Joseph's Jesuit School for Boys; and above all, St Paul's, high above Darjeeling, its lovely chapel with snow-white spire outlined against the distant snows of Kanchenjunga.

Here I was entertained to lunch with the boys (an indifferent curry, typical of school meals), by the Rector, Dr Hari Dang, and introduced to several masters, including some 'Anglos'. The boys included the *crème de la crème* of Army, princes and business. Sons of Major Generals were two a penny.

東京名所の内　乗合蒸気車往返

ohama in 1872, when Japan's first railway line from Tokyo was opened. Hiroshige's print by courtesy of Sir Hugh Cortazzi our former Ambassador to Japan

Making bullets, Darra Adem Khel

Badshahi Mosque, Lahore, Pakistan

Jamrud gate 'Gateway to the Khyber', Peshawar

President's coach and bodyguard, Rawalpindi

Kim's gun, Lahore, 'Zamzama' immortalised by Kipling

Povindahs (Nomads) on the move, Beluchistan

chak dance

s dancers in Barong dance try to stab themselves but are saved by a gic spell

Balinese Wedding, the final ceremony, bride on left

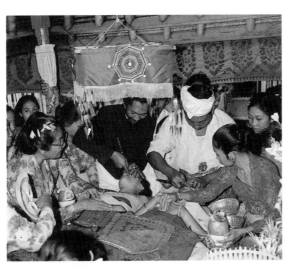

Teeth must be filed straight. Two girls submit in a ceremony

The Barong and Hanuman entertain the village children

Shwedagon Pagoda. The central spire of gold and thousands of jewels, Rangoon

Shwedagon Pagoda surrounding pagodas

Chinthe guarding entrance to Mandalay Hill

Bullocks hauling logs from River Irrawaddy, Mandalay

Buddhist Nun collecting food for her convent at Mandalay (soliciting alms is not begging, for it confers merit on the giver)

Girls worshipping at the Shwedagon

Himalayas from Nargarkot, Nepal

the 90th birthday of Brigadier Frederick Dickins, CIE.

Dhobi: Laundry in a palm grove, Mahabalipuram, Madras

Kathakali, Cochin

Rajput Finery for Basant festival

Pool of Sepahsalar Mosque, Tehran

Madresseh Madar Shah (school of the Shah's mother)

A Qashqa'i nomadic family, Shiraz

Press ups at the Zurkhaneh of Bank Melli, Te

Shah Mosque, Isfahan

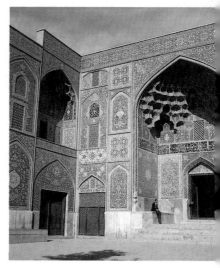

Sheikh Lotfullah Mosque, Isfahan

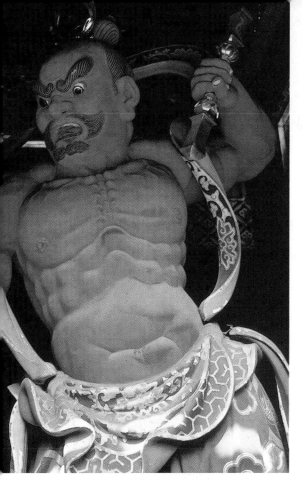

King guardian figure. Toshoga shrine, Nikko

Golden Pavilion, Kinkakuji Temple, Kyoto

F.V. Dickins, CB.

Picnic under Sakura (Cherry blossom), Kamakura

garden, Katsura Imperial Villa

Ennosuke Ichikawa, Kabuki actor

Geishas arriving at a Ryokan
(Japanese style Inn)

Michoacan Dancers in front of a Spanish Colonial Church, Mexico City

Jarabe Tapatio, regional dance of Jalisco

Pyramid of the Magician, Uxmal

India was as usual torn between rival political parties, largely based on religious or tribal differences, frequently descending into violence. In fact, the elections of 1983 brought an unusual excess of rioting, amounting (in Bihar and Assam especially) almost to civil war. Naturally the conversation veered into politics. As a representative of hated imperialism, I received short shrift. There was no question of defending imperialism; it was common ground between us that colonialism was over and done with. But in defending the Raj I did try to remind them that we had always proposed a gradual progress towards self-rule, and had actually made some concrete moves in that direction. Back in 1919, three Indians out of seven served on the Executive Council. It was just a beginning. By 1939, Congress enjoyed provincial self rule in 7 out of 11 Provinces. Not fast enough, Indians said. OK. We can agree to differ on the speed of progress, but to deny its intent is not reasonable.

The saddest thing at St Paul's was to find that for these highly intelligent and educated history masters, their history had been turned on its head, and they were quite unable to *believe* the facts, that there had ever been Congress provincial governments before and during the war. It was a Congress government that bore responsibility for the Bengal famine in 1943 – or at least *some* responsibility. Not a bit of it.

For my part, having witnessed the Bengal famine, and fought against Japanese invaders of India, what I find most distasteful is the posthumous adulation accorded to Subhas Chandra Bose, a minor politician, always opposed to Gandhi, who embraced fascism and idolised Hitler. He fled to Germany, and later to Japan, by a German submarine, where he induced 20,000 Indian prisoners of war to join the so-called Indian National Army to fight against their own country. Forty-five thousand others refused to submit, despite threats and cruelty. Bose met his death in a crashing Japanese plane. Now all over India, statues are erected to the memory of 'Netaji'; which seems to me a pathetic search for national heroes, as if India, the land of superstition, is seeking to conceal its deficiencies by the creation of new myths.

Historic facts? Ah well, it's not much use asking a blind man to open his eyes.

When Nirad Chaudhuri died in Oxford on 1 August 1999, aged 101, India lost its finest writer since Rabindranath Tagore, and its greatest savant, whose erudition covered many languages and cultures. During the war his interpretation of Britain's policies on All India Radio earned him the reputation of 'a brown Englishman'; but he was and remained equally critical of Britain's and India's follies. A pessimist on the future of mankind, he considered that the 'culture of television' would destroy all other natural cultures.

He wrote: 'Kipling was at home in our plains, hills and mountains, and like all the great novelists he remained firmly ecological... We Indians shall never cease to be grateful to Kipling for having shown the many faces of our country in all their beauty, power and truth'. Chaudhuri foresaw that the heritage of Britain would remain the dominating cultural beacon in its former Empire long after the departure of the last redcoat.

Following his *Autobiography of an Unknown Indian* in 1951, which was a literary landmark, he settled in Oxford in 1970, and continued to produce a series of books displaying his wealth of historical and philosophical knowledge until his ninety-ninth year. I have learned from all of them, including his 1,000-page second autobiography, *Thy Hand Great Anarch*. So far as India is concerned, I feel I have lost my guru.

13

A Cup of Tea for Christmas

*My salad days when I was green
in judgement, cold in blood,
to say as I said then!*

Shakespeare, *Antony and Cleopatra*

Christmas being essentially a family time, it is always sad to be spending it away from home. Nevertheless there were good reasons for extending the land voyage which changed my life, from September to February of the following year. The chief reason was the climatic factor; winter being the only time when one can be consistently comfortable in India. The second reason was that having gone to such expense of time and money, it was surely worth making a thorough job of exploring India from north to south, and incidentally including Nepal.

So Christmas 1967 was planned to be spent on a tea plantation. Tea is such a major industry of India and Sri Lanka, that it is easy to forget how young it is. Until the middle of the nineteenth century, China was the only source of tea, and the clippers of the East India Company competed to be first home with the new season's crop. Then a Mr Fortune of John Company was sent to China specifically to collect seeds and plants, and tea gardens were started in Assam and Darjeeling. (One is reminded of a similar, though secret, English endeavour, in collecting seeds of the rubber plant from Brazil.)

My choice fell on a south Indian estate at Munnar in the Palnai Hills, about 30 miles inland from the coast of Travancore State, the wealthy Hindu kingdom that fills the south-west corner of India. It is now, of course, with its neighbour, Cochin State, part of the Kerala State. About a dozen different companies, most of them English or Scottish, had plantations on these hills which reach 8,000ft, and present scenery which is a cross between Scotland and Switzerland. Through the kindness of James Finlay & Co., the Scottish merchants long established in India, I was given temporary membership of the High Range Club at Munnar, elevation 4,500ft, established by and for the benefit of the planters. The Club bungalow faces a small golf course, and has

73

a squash court, billiard room, library, and a bar whose unique decoration consists of 90 years' output of the hats of retired members, who traditionally 'hang up their hats' on retirement, with what great celebrations as can be imagined.

The valleys with their man-made lakes and steep hillsides covered with the glossy green of flat-topped tea bushes, and acres of eucalyptus (Australian blue gums) grown for fuel, are often dammed to provide irrigation and a power supply, and several lochs have been stocked with trout. There was leisure to watch the processes of tea-picking, sorting, weighing and manufacture in individual factories on each estate. The workers, who are almost all Tamils from the Madras side of the hills, much darker than the Malayalis of Kerala, have their own 'lines' of huts similar to village houses, and are provided with free water, firewood, subsidised rice, free education and health care, sports facilities, and a host of perks. By village standards they are well off, not dependent on the vagaries of the monsoon; but as you would expect, they are unionised and never satisfied. The 98-bed district hospital, with an Indian doctor, delivers 3,000 babies a year, and is well equipped, even capable of heart surgery.

During my visit there was a Tamil wedding, as fantastic and colourful a scene as you could wish. In all their brilliant multicoloured saris and jewellery, women were boiling up huge jars of rice for a feast, and two dancers had been imported, with a band of flutes and drums, to dance with heavy brass pots decorated with flowers, balanced on their heads.

Far from any town, Munnar had the peaceful atmosphere of an English village: cattle grazing in water meadows, great white bells of datura growing in hedges, under scarlet blooms of tulip trees (*spathodea*). The only unfamiliar element is the elephant. In the plains they are workers, but up here they are wild. These lovely hills are their home, and they resent man's intrusion, especially the disturbance of their long-cherished highways by modern dirt roads. They indicate their annoyance by destroying wooden shelters and signs, and frequently tear up a tea bush in order to scratch their backs with the bristly branches. They represent a danger, and we were warned, when driving at night, to be on our guard. In fact, only two weeks before my arrival, a woman and a child had been killed by elephants.

Christmas saw many preparations in the Club, Young Indian and British members were rehearsing a lively and topical revue for their New Year's Day entertainment – the predominantly Scottish element celebrate Hogmanay rather than Christmas. This was but a repetition of my childhood, when we had to make our own entertainment, and my mother was a regular participant in 'amateur theatricals'.

On Christmas Eve we had a carol service in the little stone-built church, with a congregation of about 80, many of whom of course were Indian, for in this south-western state of Kerala, over 20 per cent of the population are Christian. I was happy to receive an invitation from Lew Daltry of

Malayalam Plantations, to spend Christmas with his family. Lew's solid stone bungalow was set in a garden with well-kept lawns, gay with all the flowers of an English summer. The bungalow was built about 90 years ago by an Austrian who surrounded it with rare trees. A wood fire was roaring in the lounge, and with two bachelor planters, two mothers, the Daltrys and 8-year-old Catherine, we were a party of eight. It always feels a bit odd to be sitting down to a real English Christmas dinner of roast turkey, plum pudding and all the trimmings in so foreign a land, served by dusky servants. Or even more, serving our troops as officers must. But it is perhaps this capacity for adapting to alien surroundings while maintaining the essentials of British civilisation, that made the British Empire. As the Queen's speech came through on the radio, and we toasted 'absent friends', it took me back to a bamboo mess hut in Vizag.

Living standards have not changed since the British Raj left India; they have merely become more expensive, and are enjoyed naturally by Indians of equal rank, such as the Indian tea estate managers. It is normal for such a household to have six or seven servants. This is no luxury but a necessity, for duties are demarcated by caste and custom. Try asking your bearer to mop up a mess on the floor. He won't do it, but sends for the sweeper. For the Memsahib this may simplify life, but housekeeping is not so simple when the nearest stores are 20 miles away, and everything else must come from the local bazaar or your own produce.

A great Christmas tree stood in the hall, illuminated with fairy lights and festooned with presents, and the servants lined up for their gifts. One or two of them followed the old Indian custom, still in vogue today between father and son, or employer and employed, of kneeling down and touching the feet of their 'boss'. 'It embarrasses me,' said Lew, 'but it's their custom and I can't prevent it.' At the same time, he added that one of his gardeners was Secretary of the Trade Union which was militant on behalf of the tea workers.

Sad to relate, there is now a shortage of tea in India because Indians are drinking so much more themselves that there is not enough for export. Many British firms, including James Finlay, have pulled out of India because they can't cope with the frustrating methods of the socialist government.

All this was true of 20 years after independence; now, 52 years later, who can say? Though I constantly returned to other old haunts all over India, I never went back to Munnar. The memory was too good to lose.

14

The Festive Himalayas

Dussehra is an autumn festival which lasts ten days and honours Durga or Kali, the wife of Siva in the Hindu pantheon. Following the ceremony in Delhi where the giant effigies, 50 feet high with fearsome white faces and crowns, of the demon Ravana and his brothers Meghnath and Kumbhkarn were duly sacrificed in a joyous firework display, it was suggested that I should go up to Kulu in the foothills of the Himalayas, where the ceremony takes a different form. Kulu is one of the most beautiful mountain areas.

An agnostic Sikh taxi driver, whose parents prevented him from joining the Indian Air Force or Army which he much wanted to do, brought Moti to guide me to the Delhi ceremony. Moti was an interesting character, originally from Dera Ismail Khan, a Pathan town on the North-West Frontier. He was not a Muslim, but a Hindu refugee from partitioned Pakistan. Aged 32, he was highly educated, speaking English, French, German and several Indian languages. We were soon engaged in deep philosophical discussions on Hindu mythology and man's attitude to faith or respect for the mysteries of nature. Where else but India could you enjoy such an experience, as joyful as it was unexpected?

To reach Kulu, or Mandi as the main town is called, is quite difficult. Though there is a small airport, it has a short runway in a valley, which restricts it to small planes, and even restricts passenger numbers to 20 when the weather is bad or hot. This makes take-off difficult. A flight to Chandigarh, capital of the Punjab, with government buildings by the modernistic Le Corbusier, and a night in a government resthouse, left 180 miles to do by road to the Kulu Valley. After a quick look around the somewhat uninspiring concrete, in a taxi driven by Gur Nam Singh, we set off through the Bilaspur forest, following the Beas River valley where the Bhahkra Dam was being built.

As a result of a long and severe monsoon just ended (it was October), 100 miles of the road had been covered by gigantic landslides of earth and stones, leaving only a narrow cleared path, and this was deep in dust. So was the interior of the car, where the temperature was 94°F. Crawling between two lorries of road-building machinery, it was not a happy place. Several times, Gur Nam Singh, though as intrepid as most Sikh drivers, had to stop because he simply could not see the road. Dim recollections persist of a deep gorge with the road cut out of the mountainside above the river, but the notes I attempted to make while travelling are, understandably, mostly illegible.

Eventually we arrived, in the dark, via miles of apple orchards for which Kulu is famous (the apples are bright red, but coarse and tasteless), in a wide valley dotted with tents with a carnival atmosphere. This did not communicate itself to me when I called at the Tourist Office and found my arrival unexpected – the notification from Delhi having gone astray, as these things have a habit of doing in India. Nevertheless, I was offered a bed in the Tourist Office, and having killed a small scorpion in the bathroom, slept on a hard wooden bed. There was no shower; just a bucket to wash the dust off. Gur Nam Singh found a bed in a tent, and I invited him to use my bathroom.

He advised me that the difficulty he had been having with his gears was due to the fact that bottom gear was not working. I told him he had better find a garage or mechanic to fix it, and next day he reported, 'OK Sahib, I done fix; but now we have no reverse gear.' Somehow, this did not seem to matter; we managed. If things aren't *pukkah*, in India you must manage with *kutchah*. This wasn't the end of car troubles. Next day, we had a puncture, and the spare wheel proved to have a large chunk of rubber missing from the tread and side, exposing the inner tube. Gur Nam Singh was embarrassed when I took a picture of it, but we drove on, *kutchah* though it was.

Dussehra in Kulu involves villagers bringing in their gods for a spot of special *puja*. The gods take many forms, mostly brass idols, often artistic and of antiquity. Each village then erects a tent to house the god. The occasion is of commercial importance too, and there are hundreds of stalls selling produce or household and farming implements, or even artisans carrying out their crafts in metal or wood or cloth. Pots are re-bottomed, old biscuit tins turned into kettles: nothing, however old, is wasted in India.

The crowds number thousands; it is festival time. There are food stalls, drink stalls, an open air cinema, and for the children, swings. These are not what we know as swings, but giant wheels, 20ft high, that revolve, carrying chairs which also revolve independently. Something like Vienna's giant ferris wheel (remember Orson Welles in *The Third Man*?) on a miniaturised scale. There is a big circus tent. Police stand by with their *lathis* (brass-tipped bamboo poles), for there has been rioting. Students have been hurling manure on the State Governor and Chief Minister in protest at the half-term exams which are designed to weed out those who are slacking and will never make the grade anyway. Just like the French, always ready to enforce a demand by striking. This time in Kulu they spoilt their own fun, for they destroyed the broadcasting equipment designed to accompany the folk dancers.

Two days later, however, the folk dancers put on an excellent show, for they were competing to represent Himachal Pradesh in the great Delhi festival at Independence Day. Government authority may be ridiculed, but Rajahs are still respected, and the Rajah of Kulu was carried in procession in a palanquin, surrounded by mobile gods. The students won their demand (of course) – no intermediate exams at university. A symptom of weak government. Still, with a full moon over the mountains and the twinkling lights of the happy valley, it was a magical spot.

A few miles from Kulu is the village of Manali, in a well-forested valley containing a famous temple of Hidamba Devi which is thought to be 1,500 years old. It is built of wood, now grey with age, in the style of Norwegian stave churches. At both Manali and Kulu there were comfortable Travellers' Lodges, and Manali also offered stone-built bungalows for tourist hire, in an idyllic situation, surrounded by gardens and overlooking, from the edge of the forest, an open valley and the steep approaches to the Tibetan highlands, where Leh is the last Indian outpost.

The deodars, Himalayan cedars, are plentiful, and scent the air. A little rice is grown on terraces, and bright red corn cobs dry on rooftops. Flocks of sheep were being brought down from the high pastures for the winter, and sometimes filled the road. Once, while we waited for them to pass, a bus tried to pass us and force the sheep off the road down to the river. I soon stopped that by getting out of our car and standing in front of the bus!

Many Tibetans have escaped to India on this frontier, and some hundreds were encamped by the river Beas, surrounded by strings of prayer flags. They are very poor. The only work they can get is usually on the roads, for a few rupees a day. In winter they are snowed in, but at least they are used to this.

15

Shivering on the Equator

If anyone had told me before starting a visit to Indonesia that I would be riding a horse by moonlight at 3 a.m. across the moon-like surface of a volcanic crater, I would have said 'That's moonshine'. But it was no joke when the Jeep skittered down the rocky surface of a track hacked out of the caldera rim, and my guide announced: 'From here we make journey by horse.' Javanese horses are tiny, and the stirrups were too short, so that if I levered my six-foot frame off the saddle to ease the pain, this could only be done with bent knees. This was a fairly excruciating posture, especially with one hand occupied by looking after my three cameras, and the other by clutching a blanket round my shoulders over a tropical safari suit, to ward off bitter cold. We were just about on the Equator, but my thermometer said 46°F and there were rime crystals on the ripples of sand.

The crater of Mount Bromo is several miles wide, and our ponies were led across the crumbling surface, over some precipitous and narrow ridges, to stop at the bottom of a flight of about 100 stone steps, leading up the ridged sides of the cone – the mouth of the still active volcano. The top reaches an altitude of 6,500ft, and on the narrow rim many people were gathering to await sunrise – the object of the exercise. In a predominantly Muslim nation, the local tribe, the Tenggerese, form a tiny patch of Hindu-Buddhists, who have their own ideas of worship. This was not the day of their religious festival, Kesodo, when thousands make the pilgrimage, and throw offerings such as live chickens into the gently steaming mouth of the volcano. But there were a fair number, shivering in tropical garb, on the narrow rim, which was soft and crumbly, scarcely 6ft wide, falling away sheer on both sides. Looking down 800ft into the dark pit, Mount Bromo was puffing steam like a simmering kettle. One or two chickens were sent fluttering down to an uncertain fate.

Sunrise came with little warning; a red glow preceded the orange rays which shot above the mountain peaks, then the golden orb itself appeared, unbearable to the eye, flooding with colour the distant rim of the caldera. Now we could gauge the scale of things, and find that our Mount Bromo was just a little pussy-cat of a volcano, for the caldera, the 'sea of sand' over which we travelled the previous night, filled a crater six miles wide, in which there were two more volcano peaks. Also revealed was the immature forest growth, plants and trees, struggling to maintain a foothold on the rough volcanic surface. And a few miles away was another 12,000ft volcano, Mount Semeru.

This area of East Java, about 100 miles from Surabaya, Indonesia's second city, is the home of the Tenggerese people, who are industrious agriculturists, producing most of the vegetables which are shipped all over the country. At the attractive hill station of Tretes, where the Dutch built bungalows, amid waterfalls, cypresses and banyans inhabited by monkeys, one of the many hotels provided dinner and a few hours sleep before we drove on up to 7,000ft amid heavy traffic of *betchaks* – motorised rickshaws carrying produce to market.

Wherever you go in Indonesia you are likely to stumble across a volcano; there are hundreds of them. A short hop from Singapore across the Malacca Strait to Medan, and you are in Sumatra, an island 1,100 miles long, with 90 volcanoes. A few are still active, but in the mountainous centre, rising to 11,000ft, there is one so long dormant that it presents no threat. Way back in prehistoric times there was an eruption so vast that it created a crater 50 miles long and 20 broad. This is now Lake Toba. In the centre rises the cone, Samosir Island, which is larger than Singapore or the Isle of White. A mind-boggling scale, it remains a delightful resort, away from coastal humidity in the atmosphere of a hill station, which it was for the Dutch settlers and their coffee plantations.

It is also the centre of a tribal civilisation, the Bataks, who were in olden times in a state of constant warfare with each other, as a result of which the villages were fortified with stone walls or earth banks, planted with thickets of bamboo. And we can guess, from our experience of Japan in the war, how ingeniously the spikes of bamboo would be implanted. And that's not all about the Bataks. It must be regrettably recorded that they were cannibals until the Christian missions obtained a foothold. Today there is a strong Christian element, though of course Islam has overridden the whole of Indonesia. Of the charge of cannibalism there can be no doubt, for it was attested by Marco Polo in 1292, and by William Marsden, the chief chronicler of the history of Sumatra, in 1783. It was restricted to a punishment for criminals and POWs, but it was none the less horrifying, for the victim was carved up alive. Paradoxically, the people were literate and had their own form of writing, even in ancient times.

The Bataks are a musical and artistic race, and the villages of Samosir Island, set in the modern setting of Lake Toba with its water sports, speed-boats and a golf course, present relics of feudal kingdoms with remarkable houses, all built without nails. At Tomok, the megalithic tomb of King Sudabutar is capped with a grotesque head, and the houses are mounted on stilts 8ft high, with carved beams over a gable, roofed by an enormous sharp peak. With unhusked rice spread out to dry on tatti matting, and black swayback pigs grunting under the platforms, men sat outside with their village orchestra of gongs, cymbals, and bamboo-tube drums. For a small consideration, a few women consented to dance, an activity not conducive to fatigue, for they stood still and manipulated only their hands. I had to go as far as Fiji to see a similar performance, except that the women followed the old adage: never stand when you can sit, etc. I have always followed this advice in its entirety.

Ambarita village still retains its stone walls for defence, and outside the Chief's house is a circle of stone chairs and a round stone table, forming the court or council of war. At Pematang Purba, the longhouse of the Simalungun Batak Kings, a magnificent thatched stilt house, finely decorated, was provided with 12 hearths for his 12 wives, giving rise to the speculation whether he was offered 12 menus to choose from, or had a 12-day rota for wives. The poor chap, who has my sympathy, was assassinated in the anti-colonial revolution in 1946.

Further north at Lingga, the Karonese Bataks are a handsome pale-skinned people, whose women wear enormous hats like a flat cushion, with tassels dangling in front. Their houses are different, with blackened thatch rising to a point, topped by four gables with buffalo heads. The health resort of Brastagi is in sight of two active volcanoes, Sinabung and Sibayak. There are churches everywhere, and rice is husked communally in hollowed-out wooden beams.

16

Hanging Graves and Buffalo Feasts

The Whites always mean well when they take human fish out of the ocean and try to make them dry and warm and happy and comfortable in a chicken coop, but the kindest-hearted white man can always be depended on to prove himself inadequate when he deals with savages ... if he had any wisdom he would know that his own civilization is a hell to the savage.

Mark Twain, *Following the Equator*

If you ever had a Victorian grandparent, as I had (four of them, all living in the same village), you will have heard of an antimacassar. For the benefit of those too young to appreciate this mark of gentility, it is what airlines and some railways hang over the backs of their seats to protect them from our greasy heads. Or, to put it another way, to protect us travellers from possible contamination from the danger of headlice, the residue of previous occupants.

In Queen Victoria's time, no respectable drawing room was complete without lace antimacassars draped over the backs of armchairs. And why? Quite simple: most men smoothed their locks of hair by administering macassar oil, which was coconut oil. Indeed, right up to the outbreak of the last war, all 'matinée idols' such as Ivor Novello or film stars like Rudolf Valentino, would rather be seen dead than appear with a hair out of place. A far cry from today when a mop of hair resembling a bird's nest is accepted by all, even politicians, and even – shame to say – by girls. I was not immune to the fashionable compulsion, even as a child of, say, 9 or 10, when I begged mother to buy me some macassar oil or other unguent. Refused, I used my cricket-bat oil, which made a good substitute.

Makassar, now renamed Ujung Pandang, is a port on the island of Sulawesi, former Dutch colony of Celebes, often described in school geographies as the oddest-shaped island in the world. Its four arms are so contorted around a mountainous centre that there are poor communications between them, and each has its separate administration. South Sulawesi is the best known, for it is the home of the Toraja tribe, numbering about 300,000, who

82

inhabit Tana Toraja, the central highlands, whose forested valleys and paddy fields average around 3,000ft, with peaks rising to 11,500ft.

In the BBC religious series *The Long Search*, Torajas were chosen to illustrate Animism, though 60 per cent have been converted to Christianity. They still retain their unique burial practices, involving elaborate buffalo feasts, and interment in 'hanging graves' high up in a cliff.

To ensure a really good send-off for the deceased, it is necessary to assemble all the members of his or her family, from whatever part of the world they may be, and also to save enough money to buy and slaughter an impressive number of buffaloes, pigs and chickens. This naturally takes time, sometimes years, and it was the custom, until modern hygiene decreed otherwise, that the body should be kept at home meanwhile. For a noble, ceremonies may go on for ten days, with much feasting, drinking of palm wine, singing, dancing and watching cock fights or buffalo fights.

Only then does the burial take place, either in a cave, or for the rich, in specially excavated tombs, the 'hanging graves', high up in the face of a sheer cliff. Ladders of bamboo are required to carry the corpse up; and then in some cases, a balcony is carved out of the cliff, on which almost life-size effigies of the dead man or woman, fully dressed, stand guard. Poorer citizens make do with natural caves, where the coffins are lodged in crevices to rot away slowly and eventually disgorge their load of bones and skulls which remain scattered about.

Toraja art is distinctive, based on the traditional house design: three storeys and verandah, raised on stilts, the peaks (front and rear) soaring up like the prow of a ship, with a marked overhang supported by a 60ft kingpost, into which hammer beams are slotted to support the sides. The whole is covered with bamboos arranged in organ-pipe patterns, with thatch upon these. Every inch of the beams and the front is carved and painted with tribal designs in red, yellow, white and black. No nails are used. For decoration, many buffalo horns, each representing a funeral feast and denoting wealth. Grain-stores are made in the same style, but smaller. It is a culture which bespeaks stability and prosperity and the people are very pleasant and friendly.

The coastal Bugis tribe are noted sailors, responsible for most of the inter-island trade, though they also had a reputation in the past as pirates. I met several of them with their heavy wooden *pinisis* and they were amiable enough to invite me on board, though we had no common language. The crew of 14 were having a meal on deck. There must have been 100 of the heavy craft with great solid bowsprits jutting forward, and high masts supported by wooden ladders instead of shrouds. They were loading or unloading timber and cement. Lawrence and Lorne Blair, who wrote the book *Ring of Fire* and presented the BBC series on their travels through the Spice Islands, describe their four-month voyage as passengers in one of these ships. The book is not only hilarious, but an excellent introduction to the tribal way of life in Indonesia.

It is an eight-hour road journey from Tana Toraja to Ujung Pandang, in order to fly out of South Sulawesi, and due to flight schedules an overnight stay is unavoidable. Fort Rotterdam, the seventeenth-century Dutch fort which protected their sea route to the Spice Islands, the Moluccas, has been well restored. The Grand Hotel offered comfort on a par with the old Raffles in Singapore, its white arched colonnades surrounding a garden courtyard. My suite consisted of sitting room, bedroom and bathroom, and on opening the door a swarm of mosquitoes arose, buzzing to do battle. After the room boy vigorously sprayed every corner, their reserves entered the fray. After tracking down the last guerilla survivors and picking stupefied warriors off the bed, the night was undisturbed, provided I opened and shut the door quickly enough to foil fresh invaders.

In Makassar I went to bed with a 'Dutch wife'. Not quite what it sounds, but an invention of the sybaritic Dutch from the days when *punkahs* were the only source of a cooling draught. It consists of a short bolster placed in the middle of the bed, round which you twine your legs to prevent them sticking together with sweat. The Grand Hotel provided one.

17

An Island of Tribes

'Like a wild man of Borneo' was an epithet current in Victorian times, reflecting the unknown but reputedly savage character of this, the third largest island in the world. Few in Britain know or care where Borneo is, but it has produced both the richest man in the world and jungle-living tribes whose manhood is expressed by head-hunting, the trophies of which still adorn their longhouses. Oil and timber have been the sources of its wealth, and British soldiers have known what it is to fight a guerilla enemy through monsoons in the leech- and mosquito-infested jungles.

The huge island lies just a few miles off Singapore, and shares its relentlessly humid climate. It is divided politically on a roughly east-west axis, the lower two thirds being Kalimantan and belonging to Indonesia. The northern coasts reflect colonial growth through the states of Sarawak and Sabah, constituting East Malaysia, and the Sultanate of Brunei, where dwells that wealthy autocrat. All three have an interesting history. Sabah was once the British North Borneo Company, a purely commercial operation, funded by the City of London. Historically, Brunei was the ruling Sultanate which claimed Suzerainty over the whole island. Thanks to the fiercely independent Dyak tribes and the Sulu sea pirates who preyed on shipping, the Brunei Sultans of the nineteenth century exercised only a nebulous control over their feudal 'Pengirans' or nobles, and were seldom able to collect taxes much outside their capital. The capricious Sultan of 1841 ceded to James Brooke the territory of Sarawak, nearly as large as England, in return for help in suppressing piracy. Thus began the reign of the 'White Rajahs' which lasted until 1946.

All three territories gained from Britain the rule of law and the suppression of piracy and slavery. When I visited Brunei 30 years ago, it was still a British Protected State. Today it resembles Singapore in modernity, orderliness and prosperity. Its citizens enjoy low taxes and excellent social services. A helicopter of the Malay Regiment flew me with a civilian doctor on a regular visit to a village deep in the jungle. The same trip gave me a striking poster for British Airways of the newly-built Mosque, a £10 million vision of white and gold, that dominates the capital city, Bandar Seri Begawan. It stands in the middle of the Kampong Ayer or Water Village, a shallow lagoon where 20,000 people live in wooden houses supported on flimsy-looking piles, joined by wooden walkways. Primitive though these dwellings appear, they are quite comfortable inside, and the tenants resist all suggestions that they might transfer to terra firma. One reason may be that they pay no rent. Tiny children leap from verandahs into the murky water, and market women paddle canoes with produce for sale.

It was Sir Omar Ali Saifuddin, the father of the present Sultan, who steered Brunei into the modern world in 1950. He was a fervent admirer of Sir Winston Churchill, and built the superb Memorial Museum, a semicircular building with a statue of Sir Winston outside. Inside, it surveys his life from boyhood to death. Realistic dioramas show the boy at Harrow, reading in camp on the North-West Frontier, charging at the battle of Omdurman, and as a captive of the Boers. Recorded voices of Churchill's wartime exhortations, with a sound-and-light version of the London Blitz, make an inspiring tribute.

Another magnificent museum is devoted to the arts and artifacts of tribal Borneo, such as costumes made from the feathers of the sacred hornbill, cannons in the shape of crocodiles and dragons, and Chinese ceramic jars dating back to the Han era. The museum was opened by the Queen in 1972.

Recently the Sultan has built a vast and sumptuous new palace, with separate palaces for his four wives. It is open to the public on one day a year, the festival of Id, marking the end of Ramadan.

Where stands the richest autocrat in the world today? Oil revenues are crumbling, and a playboy reputation sullies the 'royal' family. Brunei has every reason to thank the battalion of Gurkhas who protect its wealth at the Seria oilfields.

There could not be a greater contrast than the quiet and sleepy atmosphere of Sarawak, where the stately white columns and pediment of the White Rajah's Courts of Justice dominate the capital, Kuching, while the low yellow buildings of James Brooke's Palace lie on the opposite side of the river. Chinese 'shophouses' provide small-time commerce, but the real business lies up country in the jungles where the industrialisation of Asia demands the sacrifice of age-old forests to logging firms. Despite attempts to control the stripping of trees, the whole of Borneo, including the Indonesian part, is being steadily denuded of timber. Fires have recently added to the destruction, covering millions of square miles with dense smoke. Saddest of all losers are the human-like orang utans, who are being threatened with extinction by deprivation of living space – trees.

A short excursion up-river introduced me to a Dyak longhouse, the long thatched wooden platform, about 10ft high, containing about 20 individual homes. Life is not communal, though the outer slatted platform or verandah is shared by all. Shrivelled skulls decorated the eaves, and trunks of coconut palms were notched to form steps up to the platform. Swarms of children played in the river, and one girl carried water home in a bamboo tube.

The 200 tribes of Borneo are but a microcosm of the vastly greater number of tribes that make up South East Asia as a whole and give it its fascinating variety. From India to China, the many countries whose names are inscribed on the map conceal the greatest diversity of people in the world. The biggest mistake the West makes is to think that a name on a map represents a coherent tribe – if only because many different races are involved, and religions too. If we include, as we should, northern Australia in South East Asia, we can see tribes in all stages of development from the most primitive hunter gatherers, animists and spirit worshippers, to the highly intelligent, scientifically educated scholars and businessmen of India and China. When does a tribe become a country or a nation? Only when it is 'westernised'? Not necessarily so, for nothing could be more brutally tribal then the Serbs and Albanians of the Balkans. So tribal feelings survive even 'civilisation'.

The French had a system, born of their colonial past, of classifying the tribal people whom they took under their wing in the most primitive parts of Africa. First they must be *apprivoisé* (tamed), then later they are *assimilé* (assimilated) when they adopt western ways of dress, education and living. I saw examples in the Caribbean islands of Guadeloupe and Martinique, obviously *bien assimilé*, and the tiny colony of Mahé, one of France's four Indian colonies – now of course abolished. During a leave in 1942 when I explored the Malabar coast by local buses, I came across this enclave, a speck of sandy beach, sweltering under a canopy of coconuts, indistinguishable from the rest of Kerala, where the barefooted fishermen and coconut farmers were French citizens, *with a vote*. France was ahead of us here. The French Administrator, Monsieur Boué, who lived here with his Parisian wife, entertained me to a fresh coconut drink under the Croix de Lorraine, and proudly told me that they had universal education, voted for a Deputy to the French Parliament, and had provided 1,500 volunteers for the Free French Forces.

What has this to do with Borneo? Not a lot, except to remind us that tribalism is not a matter of race or religion, but overrides all political changes. The British tribe has been invaded by Romans, Saxons, Danes and Norse, but it is highly improbable that it will ever think of itself as a 'European' tribe. Whether it can be destroyed as a tribe by overwhelming dilution by other tribes is another matter.

18

The Jungle Cities of Angkor

Ah Love! Could thou and I with Fate conspire
to grasp this sorry Scheme of Things entire,
Would not we shatter it to bits – and then
Re-mould it nearer to the heart's desire?

The Rubaiyat of Omar Khayyam, Stanza 73

Forty years ago, Norodom Sihanouk, self-proclaimed King of Cambodia, entertained Malcolm Macdonald, Britain's Commissioner General in South East Asia, in his kingdom. In his book *Angkor* Macdonald describes the sumptuous meals of both western and oriental viands. Whether in the palace or on a picnic, the champagne was always well-cooled, and the Rolls Royce always available to transport the guest from a seaside guesthouse to the distant jungles, where the past glories of the Khmer nation lay exposed in ruins. Temples, monasteries, libraries, canals and tanks, giant arches, causeways, walls expressing in graphic low relief the daily life, the armies and the battles of the Khmers and their enemies the Siamese and the Chams (Vietnamese). So well did the ruins lie concealed by the all-enveloping jungle after they were abandoned in 1432 that it was not until 1860 that they were 'discovered' and publicised by Frenchman Henri Mouhot.

It is not strictly accurate to speak of 'discovering' Angkor, for previous visitors include the Chinese diplomat Chou Ta Kuan who stayed from 1296–1297 and wrote extensively about it; and a Portuguese, Diego do Conto, who described Angkor Wat in 1614. But let that pass. We Europeans like to think that we discovered all the rest of the world.

Since 1860, jungle clearance and restoration have revealed an astonishing achievement of not one, but several distinct cities representing the capitals of successive rulers, whose origins from the Javanese Sailendra dynasty (origin-ally from India) were Hindu, but soon became overlaid by Buddhism. The buildings reflect clearly the two religions side by side. An inventory taken by the greatest builder of all, Jayavarman VII in 1181, records that there were 102 hospitals and 121 resthouses for pilgrims. Naturally such enormous projects required slave labour, for more stone was used in Angkor than in the Great Pyramid of Khafre (Kufu) in Egypt. One Khmer temple alone required the population of 3,000 villages to construct. Besides which, standing armies were maintained and equipped with spears and shields, and war elephants. Low-relief galleries half a mile long tell the story like a strip cartoon, but with supreme artistry. All was made possible by a climate, aided by irrigation, that produced three crops of rice per year.

That such a promising economy and proved capacity for building should have crumbled to the farce of Sihanouk and the horror of the Khmer Rouge, is one of the tragedies of history. The self-indulgence of Sihanouk, his baffling changes of mind, at one time abdicating in favour of his father, at another joining the Khmer Rouge, and again resuming autocratic power as Head of State, may have justified some left-wing unrest. But none could have imagined the excesses of Pol Pot. With the express intention of destroying civilisation as we knew it, and of 'turning the clock back to year zero', whole cities were emptied of their population without a moment's notice; money was destroyed, books, science and medicine vandalised; and millions of people sent to fend for themselves in the countryside, to subsist by growing rice. Pol Pot's legacy is storehouses of skulls and bones, and a million landmines which still ensure the mutilation of thousands of peaceful peasants, as Cambodia struggles to reanimate a civilisation that created one of the true 'Wonders of the World'.

I visited Phnom Penh 12 years after Macdonald's visit and one year before Pol Pot's regime, when it was a clean, modern city: the Hotel Royale displaying all the marks of a French civilisation; good coffee and croissants, and service 'comme il faut'. The hotel's swimming pool was fragrant with frangipani, hibiscus and bougainvillaea. Local women wore either black silk trousers if they were Vietnamese, or long black sarongs, some to ankles, some to calf, if they were Khmer. Hundreds of cyclo-pousses pedalled past. Men carried baskets of vegetables slung on bamboo poles. Strolling through the city with its fine French houses and gardens, and a temple on a hill where joss-sticks burned and fortune tellers sat around, I wandered in the market where fish were drying on stone benches, and stopped at a café for iced tea. It was only about 85°, but sticky.

Next morning Cambodia Travel Service had a city tour by bus, but as I was the only passenger, they sent a car instead, which was pretty decent of them. First stop was the Royal Palace on the banks of the Mekong, where several orange-clad Bhikkus were passing by. The royal jewels in the Museum were dazzling, as were the gifts of the bejewelled Buddhas; one diamond ornamented a bowler hat. The throne room, built in 1915, had a marble floor, painted ceiling dome and nave like a church; one throne for the King and another behind for the Queen had been used only once. The French were masters of 'indirect rule'. The separate Queen's palace had reception halls and a dancing hall which was used every day, for Sihanouk was very keen on keeping alive the court dances and costumes which are perpetuated in Tourist

Thailand today. His daughters were accomplished dancers. They may well have been among the dazzling performers of the Royal Ballet which I photographed in the innermost sanctums of Angkor Wat the next evening.

It took an hour in an ancient but very clean Dakota to transfer to Siem Reap's modern airport, where the bus deposits the visitor at the very entrance to the Wat, i.e. the Temple of Angkor, in the aptly named 'Auberge des Temples', air-conditioned and with swimming pool. In such ancient cities you might look for a royal palace, but you will find none, for the royal residences were all built of wood, which has rotted away in the 600 years of surrender to nature. Every building is a temple or part of one, for each successive Hindu ruler sought to construct his own Mount Meru, the five-towered mountain which is the cosmic centre of the Hindu universe, and home of the gods. The two best-preserved temples are Angkor Wat itself, and the Bayon, the central temple of the later city Angkor Thom.

So extensive are the ruins (they cover 60 square miles) that motor transport is required to see more than a casual sample. Many locals had devised motorised rickshaws, and a particularly ingenious Mr Yi Huon had arranged a fairly comfortable low chair on wheels, which he towed behind his two-stroke motor bike. It was exhilaratingly cool as we whizzed along at 20mph on jungle roads which were well-graded, and even marked with the standard French red and white stones for main roads.

The buildings, erected over a period of four centuries, and neglected for six more, vary in their state of repair, but all show the Khmer passion for detail and perfection, even in inaccessible places which cannot be seen. The general pattern involves pyramidal forms, representing Mount Meru, sometimes rising to 200ft, as at Ta Keo. At Angkor Wat, long corridors with barred windows lead to outlying pavilions and terraces, rising to the central pyramid's final 37 steps of such steep pitch that it is really difficult (and dangerous) to negotiate them. Every inch of the building is covered with delicate sculpture, gods and Apsaras, the heavenly maidens with triple crowns, flowing skirts, and jewelled necklaces and girdles, celestial dancers who rewards the faithful in heaven. Both at Angkor Wat and the Bayon are walls extending for thousands of yards, filled with a detailed history of battles, as well as homely scenes of daily life: a mother playing with her children, or grilling fish, a man lighting a fire and kneeling down to blow on it. Marching armies of Khmers trample over their defeated enemies, commanded by their officers mounted on chariots or elephants. There are sea battles, with a crocodile devouring a man thrown in the water.

The massive temple of the Bayon has 49 towers, built of blocks of stone, sculpted to show huge smiling faces on each of the four sides. At first these were thought to be Bodhisattvas, Buddhist saints who have attained Nirvana, but elected to remain earthbound in order to help humanity achieve Nirvana too. Now, however, they are thought to represent King Jayavarman VII, the greatest builder of the Bayon itself and eight other temples.

On the Bayon, the Apsaras have reached their most fanciful flowering, dancing two or three at a time, on lotus flowers. More usually, they stand erect and single, hands and flowing skirts indicating the movement of a dance. They may be found almost anywhere; at a doorway, or high up on the topmost walls of Angkor Wat. Intricate finger movements are today continued in the dances of Thailand and Bali.

Entrances to the walled city of Angkor Thom are through high arches with triple peaks, approached by a causeway 100 yards long, guarded by two Nagas (the mythical snake which symbolises the bridge between earth and heaven). Massive stone figures, on one side of demons, on the other side of gods, are hauling on the snakes. This represents in Hindu mythology the pulling in alternate directions of the giant snake Vasuki, which is wound round Mount Mandara, resting on a turtle in the Sea of Milk, which is churned by the motion to produce *amrita*, the elixir of life or immortality.

Water is essential to a rice economy, and Cambodia is fortunate in the freak condition whereby the flow of the Mekong is impeded by sandbanks in the estuary, forcing a reversing of its flow during the monsoon, to inflate the huge lake of Tonle Sap which lies alongside the river and joins it just below Phnom Penh. Not content with this, the Khmer Kings built vast waterworks, canals and 'barays' which ensured great fertility. One such lake, the Sras Srang, was the King's bathing place, and nearby is a village of houses on stilts. Here one meets the local population: Buddhist monks in a recently-build monastery; a little girl of about 10, carrying water from the lake in two palm-leaf buckets suspended from a bamboo pole; an elephant receives her daily bath. A peaceful scene, unfortunately 30 years ago. Today, who knows? Access is free; but danger lurks from mines, bandits and the odd shot from the Khmer Rouge.

Reclamation from the jungle and restoration of the temples has continued, with archaeologists from many countries interested. Two sites have deliberately been left uncleared, to indicate the state in which they were found. These are Preah Khan and Ta Promh. Here the jumble of giant building stones, first laterite, then later sandstone, lie under enveloping lianas, creepers, and relentless trees which have literally torn the buildings apart. Chief of these is the strangler fig, which often grows from seeds dropped by birds in the branches or on the summits of buildings, spreading downward with many earth-seeking roots until it envelops and kills the tree or building. Equally deadly is the kapok or silk cotton tree, whose above-ground roots swell to enormous sizes, the diameter of a man's body, forcing entry as a tiny root through the smallest crack in building blocks, then swelling to split them apart. Yet others, forest giants 100 feet high, develop huge sideways buttresses which simply ride over any man-made obstacle. The power of nature is frightening. Here and there, glimpses through the undergrowth show a grinning

Bodhisattva face, a lovely Apsara, a barred window or a superbly carved lintel to a doorway. Man's art carelessly destroyed. As Keynes remarked, 'In the long run, we are all dead'.

19

Barefoot on a Hot Gold Pagoda

By the old Moulmein Pagoda, lookin' eastward to the sea,
There's a Burma girl a-setting', an' I know she thinks of me;
For the wind is in the palm-trees, as the temple bells they say:
'Come you back, you British soldier; come you back to Mandalay!'
Come you back to Mandalay,
Where the old flotilla lay.
Can't you 'ear their paddles chunkin' from Rangoon to Mandalay?
On the road to Mandalay,
Where the flyin'-fishes play,
An' the dawn comes up like thunder outer China
'Crost the Bay.

Kipling, 'Mandalay'

There's no option if you visit the Shwe Dagon Pagoda in Rangoon. It's shoes *and* socks off; and boy, is it hot on the sun-drenched marble platform surrounding the towering gold spire, reputed to contain 25 tons of gold, and 100 of silver. Damaged by an earthquake in 1930, its *hti* (the umbrella which tops many Burmese pagodas) was replaced with one inlaid with 6,000 diamonds, emeralds and rubies. Its summit is slightly higher than St Paul's Cathedral.

Painful to the feet it may be, but what takes the breath away is the rich decoration of the multicoloured pavilions, tapering spires of scarlet or gold, prayer halls and shrines containing multiple Buddha statues, fretwork wooden lattice screens and stepped pyramids, the upturned corner of which reflect their Chinese counterparts.

The Shwe Dagon Pagoda is the most sacred place of pilgrimage, because it contains eight hairs of Gautama Buddha. It was probably built about 588 BC. All the small altars, pinnacles and pavilions were erected by Buddhist patrons as a mark of religious piety, to 'gain merit' – an indulgence which *can* be bought. Surely a negation of the true philosophy of Buddhism?

In the bazaars one can find professional gold beaters, hammering away at little packets of gold encased in leather, to produce 1,000 sheets of wafer-thin gold leaf, no weightier than a postage stamp, which the poor can buy for a few pence and affix to any religious statue or building to 'gain merit'. Millionaires of course can donate another pagoda.

Rangoon's Strand Hotel was once as smart and fashionable as Singapore's Raffles. Did my mum and dad ever dine and dance there on short leave from their outstation posting, I know not where? They would not care for its dreary style today, on the muddy river bank.

Britain fought three Burma Wars between 1824 and 1885 to add this lovely country to our Empire, originally as part of India, and granted its independence in 1948, just one year after India's. Burma had a 1,000-year history of rule by kings, expanding into the northern reaches of the Irrawaddy, and not infrequently tangling with their Thai neighbours over the bordering Shan States (now the 'Golden Triangle' of opium cultivation and drug smuggling). This is the root cause of the instability which dogs the reputation of Myanmar (the modern name), for they have a civil war on their hands in the struggle for independence by Shans, Karens and Kachins, mixed up with attempts at suppressing the drug traffic, in which there is a strong suspicion that government officials themselves have taken over the lucrative role of 'drug barons' such as Khun Sa.

Burma's kings were a mixed lot. In 1044 Anawrahta ruled at Pagan, and introduced Buddhism. The capital shifted to Pegu, Ava, and finally Mandalay. In the long and peaceful rule of King Mindon, good relations were established with Britain for 25 years, but he was followed by King Thibaw, a monster who murdered all his relatives and was plainly insane. He was deposed in 1885 and exiled. His tyranny provided the excuse for the third Burma War and English rule. So it is a very different history from India's.

Pagan was conquered by Kublai Khan in 1287, and Marco Polo passed this way about the same time, noting that the temples were built by free men, and the women were also free and equal. They still are, keeping their name and property rights on marriage, except for Aung San Suu Kyi, who won an election but was denied office by the Army and kept under house arrest, even when her British husband was dying.

Pagan was reputed to have 13,000 temples or pagodas at one time, spread over 20 miles of the Irrawaddy, the great highway of commerce which flowed past my hotel garden with gay banks of bougainvillaea. Teams of bullocks strained to haul out huge trunks of trees that floated down from logging camps in the far north. Teak and mahogany represented a good part of Burma's wealth; rice and precious stones, rubies especially, the rest.

Pagan was severely damaged in an earthquake in 1975, but a few hundred pagodas remain, of which the most elaborately decorated is the Shwezigon, many of whose tapering spires are made of carved wood. The Ananda Pagoda has four 30ft-high Buddhas, built in the eleventh century. Villages consisted of houses made from wood, built on stilts with palm-leaf thatch, and bullock carts plodding along earth roads. In the bazaars women wore slender *lunghis* and tight jackets, often smoking fat cheroots, their hair decked with flowers. An amiable, laid-back lifestyle pervades the countryside, but they have festivals on full moon days, especially on their New Year when a water-sprinkling ceremony ensures that everybody gets west. Best to avoid.

It was King Mindon who built Mandalay Fort, a square of high red-brick crenellated walls, each one mile long, inside a wide moat and pallisaded walls. Twelve entrances by causeways across the moat are marked by gateways with ornate pagodas of whitewashed walls and tapering spires of carved teak. The palace in the centre was the Japanese headquarters during the war, and thus destroyed by air and land bombardment when we recovered Burma in 1945. Though rebuilt, it is not open to visitors.

No 'flying fishes play' in Mandalay, but it has a surfeit of pagodas, of which the most important for religious reasons is the Kuthodaw, consisting of 729 small white *stupas* enclosed within a white wall, each containing a page of Buddhist scripture; and a central gilded spire. Another is the Mahamya Mouni, with a large Buddha statue in its inner sanctum, covered with gold leaf several inches thick, the face being left silver. At the Shwe Nandaw, of intricately carved wood, once gilded all over, three little boys in the robes of a *ponggyi* were in attendance; for it is customary for children or young men to spend some months as monks, as part of their religious upbringing. Mandalay Hill, which towers steeply above the city, is guarded by a pair of 20ft-high *chinthes*, (white lion-dragons), which seem to be challenging the visitor to undertake the exhausting climb, which takes 45 minutes.

Taunggyi, on the borders of the Shan hill states, is a hill station at 4,800ft, cool enough for log fires. It is also a military headquarters, and a measure of the instability caused by independence movements was the armed soldier who stood on guard outside our hotel all night, and two on the airport roof at Heho.

Our objective, the Inle Lake, is an enchanting spot, nine miles long and four broad, and noted for two things. One is the village which floats on the lake, partly on stilts, and partly on the compressed vegetation which is dredged from the lake bottom, forming a solid enough base to support houses, schools and pagodas. Dugout canoes with outboard motors took parties of eight on a tour which showed us the unique feature: the leg rowers. They stand on one leg at the end of a canoe, and wrap the other leg around an oar in order to row. It sounds uncomfortable, but is highly effective, and even small boys were legging themselves to school in small canoes. The system of dredging rotted vegetation to form fresh soil is also employed in Kashmir on Dal Lake, and provides a rich manure on which trees grow.

In the village (on land) children presented us with necklaces made from lotus buds, and men were playing *chinlon*, a ball game using a light wicker-work ball which must be kept in the air as long as possible, using only feet, elbows, knees, shoulders and heads; anything but hands. Extraordinary skill was displayed, especially in kicking the ball from behind with the back of the heel.

In the bazaar a group of Buddhist nuns with silver bowls on their shaven heads were going the rounds of collecting their daily food (rice and vegetables) for their two meals a day, before midday. This should not be confused with begging, for they are doing a kindness to the laymen by giving them an opportunity to 'gain merit' by giving alms.

20

Elephant round-up

One elephant – a new elephant – an elephant's child – who was full of 'satiable curiosity.

'How the Elephant Got His Trunk', Kipling, *Just So Stories*

Bangkok is one of those cities, like Hong Kong or Singapore, that always seems to be on the route to wherever you are visiting in Asia. As a city it is unrivalled for its wealth of colourful *wats*, its royal palace, and its picturesque *klongs* which are arteries of waterborne commerce. Moreover, as a kingdom which has never felt the alien hand of colonialism, but has had an independent role in the often warlike history of its neighbours Burma and Cambodia, its gentle Buddhist people are among the most agreeable of South-East Asia.

Its very popularity as a tourist centre has led to gross traffic congestion and pollution, so that, after many visits to record the religious buildings and traditional folk dances, it now seems preferable to look outside the city. Up country to Chieng Mai and other places of the 'Golden Triangle' of poppy production, near the border of Laos, yields a rather different variety of tribal people, each with their own costume, language and religion which is usually more Animist than Buddhist. As everywhere in the East, the concept of spirits, inherent in every object be it human, animal or earthly (the Japanese *kami*), which we of the West find it so hard to comprehend, rules people's lives. Thus a tribesman shooting a wild deer for food may make an offering to the animal's spirit – for spirits must be respected. If offended, they could do harm. It is this concept which accounts for so much of the misunderstanding between East and West.

I certainly respect the 'spirit' of elephants, that most intelligent of animals, and in the forests of Thailand they are man's best friend, performing feats of strength and intelligence that can be done no better by machinery. Sadly, the latest news from Thailand is that in response to worldwide cries to end the denudation of forests which is rapidly changing the climate and destroying the habitat of many endangered species, all further logging has been stopped.

97

As a result, thousands of elephants have joined the ranks of the unemployed, and their *mahouts* or *ouzies* with them.

A notice advertising an 'Elephant Round-up Festival' at Surin in north-east Thailand was quite enough to send me hot on the trail. An excursion was organised by TAT: the Tourism Authority of Thailand, with a special train of modern, all metal sleeping cars. Upper and lower berths ran *along* the coaches rather than transversing them, with curtains for privacy, and aluminium ladders to climb up. Toilets and washbasins had running water, and the bedding was clean.

It was intolerably stuffy in Bangkok, but once we got going on the nine-hour journey it was quite comfortable on my lower berth with the barred window open. The upper berth was not so lucky. Next day at Surin, the afternoon shade temperature was 87°F, but without the humidity of Bangkok it was quite bearable.

The Sirinthorn Secondary School had been prepared to receive us visitors, and the open-sided auditorium was laid out for breakfast of soup, rice and chicken, served by some of the 2,000 students. The girls appeared again that evening, dressed in long Thai silk skirts and blouses, to guide us through the intricacies of a Thai dinner, sitting uncomfortably on tatami mats, with food in chased silver bowls, set out with many dishes on low bamboo stools. The girls and boys ended with a display of folk dancing fully equal to the professionals of Bangkok restaurants and night clubs.

Two hundred of our elephant friends were waiting for us on a huge arena between grandstands, and we were on the Press platform, for three different TV companies were doing a programme: one from Alaska, one from Canada, and one from the Thai Open University. The Grand Parade marched around the arena. There were many mothers with their children, for elephants having the same life span as humans, babies depend on their mothers for suckling and defence to well over 2 years. Three were too young to parade, and remained in the centre with their mothers. The youngest was only 19 days old, and when a dog approached, barking, it was lovely to see the maternal care with which the mother shepherded the baby underneath her, and reassured it with gentle touches of the trunk.

A real round-up, as in a forest, could hardly be expected, but there was a demonstration of how it is done. The catchers are specially trained elephants, mounted by men with a noose on the end of a pole, and ropes of buffalo hide. Young elephants were chased down the field and lassoed by the catchers. It is surprising how fast they can run.

Our elephants came from a training school for work in the teak forests, and their cleverness was demonstrated in several ways. Six men lay down in a row, and six elephants in procession stepped carefully over them. So long as their front legs are placed right, the hind ones follow automatically. They also walked along planks.

Races between teenager elephants involved placing a dozen bottles in a line, and the young ones had to run and collect the bottles one by one and bring them back to the starting line. This was quite strenuous in the afternoon heat, when they would have preferred to be cooling off in their baths. Most ran with a will, but one got bored after ten bottles, and plainly said to his *mahout*, 'I've had enough of this silly game. You pick it up yourself.'

Finally, there was a spectacular parade of war elephants, fitted with *howdahs* carrying men armed with spears and swords. About 30 lined up for inspection by the 'King' in a gorgeous *howdah* with a tapered pagoda of white globes above him. Squads of footmen in uniforms of red, green and black, armed with medieval-looking broadswords and pikes, manoeuvred against other uniformed men; and after a formal review of his 'Army', the 'King' and his merry *mahouts* and their tanks advanced along the arena, and staged a battle with sparks flashing from clashing swords.

In the tug of war, one old matriarch was set against a squad of soldiers. Thirty she pulled over with ease; 140 men she defeated, but not without strain. A football match was plainly enjoyed, especially by the teenagers.

21

Chosun: Land of Morning Calm

In three days, fish — and guests — stink.

Chinese proverb

Korea has some similarities with Japan, which it might not please a Japanese to hear, but the likeness of a mountainous and very beautiful countryside is undeniable. Lying between China and Japan, Korea is often thought of by historians as the conduit of Chinese culture to Japan, but Koreans would stoutly maintain that whatever arts they may have passed on, they are their own. Obviously there are links between all three countries, but compared to the secretive and inward-looking history of Japan, Korea's is well-documented right back to before the Christian era.

Until the present century, Korea has always been a kingdom; counting its origins from the Three Kingdom era, comprising the Silla from 57 BC, the Koguryo from 37 BC and the Paekche from 18 BC, each in different areas of the peninsula, which is now split by the Korean War, leaving the north half a silent desert of communism, bisected by a farcical border of play-acting.

The intervening years have seen many changes of power, and invasions by the Mongols and by the Japanese Shogun Hideyoshi, who laid waste the land as far north as Seoul, but was soon defeated at sea by the brilliant Korean Admiral Yi-Sun-shin. Ever inventive, the Koreans already had, in 1592, iron-clad ships called 'turtles'. Further invasions from Manchuria drove Korea into a period of isolation when the West was debarred, and Christians were persecuted. It was known as the 'Hermit Kingdom'. Finally, there was subjection to Japan from 1910 until the end of the Second World War in 1945.

The first thing you notice in Korea is the writing on signboards and advertisements; it is neither Chinese nor Japanese nor any other of the multitude of Asian languages. It is Korean, and written in the unique *han'gul* alphabet which was invented by King Sejong who ruled from 1418 to 1450. It is the world's first phonetic alphabet.

Though already ancient when Columbus 'discovered' America, Seoul is now a thoroughly modern city of 8 million people, built as a walled city with nine gates, of which five remain. What makes Seoul such a beautiful city is the multitude of royal palaces, most of which have been destroyed and rebuilt at various times, but now form a complex of parks, lakes and pleasure grounds, right in the heart of the city.

The main throne hall of Changdok Palace is a low two-storey pavilion with upturned tile roof, and panels of pierced screens on the front. Like all the historic buildings, the most lavish decoration is built into the eaves which are a mass of highly intricate and multi-coloured patterns. They are built without nails; wood and tiles fitted together. Some feature pagodas of three or five storeys upon a stone base. One, the Kyonghoeru Pavilion, is an open-sided banqueting house, standing on a lake. Other lakes and small pavilions form a wild area known as the 'Secret Garden'.

The last King, Sunjong, who abdicated when Japan annexed Korea in 1910, continued to live in Changdok Palace until his death in 1926, and his widow Queen Yun and the Crown Prince's widow lived in the annex of Naksonjae until their deaths in 1966 and 1970 respectively. So the royal connection is very recent; though there is not the same profound respect for Korean royalty as there is for the Japanese Emperor.

I was very lucky to encounter in the grounds of Changdok Palace, the Royal Band, in costumes of yellow with stove-pipe hats, practising with long trumpets, drums and cymbals. Only recently have the Secret Garden's 78 acres been opened to the public, and tradition tells of 'unbelievable orgies' of a former prodigal King Yonsan-gun, featuring nymphs dancing in the woods and on the terraces beside sylvan ponds. It is quite a thought, in relation to Hyde Park, the Bois de Boulogne, or the Tiergarten.

So conscious is Korea of its national culture, that it has listed and numbered all the most notable 'national treasures', be they buildings, statues, paintings, bells, golden crowns or whatever; though not, as in Japan, people. Yes, you can be a 'national treasure' for your accomplishments there while still alive. I wonder how the idea would fit in for us? I can think of quite a few people who would *not* qualify.

The National Museum in Seoul has a lot to celebrate: a large iron Buddha of the eleventh century; a gilt bronze smiling Maitreya with one leg crossed over the knee, from the seventh century; a marble Bodhisattva of the tenth century; the Celadon ware of the Koryo dynasty is twelfth century and Buddhist, the porcelain of the eighteenth century Yi dynasty is Confucian. For religion changed over the centuries, with elements of Shamanism and belief in spirits (as in Japan) merging with Buddhism and Confucianism. The latter element accounts for the great emphasis on learning and discipline that makes Koreans such hard workers.

Then there is the Folklore Museum, exhibiting the traditional methods of building, the tools of agriculture, the costumes, food, furnishings and transport, as they were. These are nicely illustrated by waxwork models: one showing ploughing with an ox, another a home scene with a richly-gowned

101

daughter being taught by a father with the wispy beard and pointed stove-pipe hat that typifies old Korea.

This theme is carried to perfection in the Korean Folk Village about 25 miles out of Seoul. Here an entire river valley has been turned into a living museum of houses, from simple thatched cottages to elaborate manors, and a Provincial Governor's Palace. Most traditional homes consisted of a group of buildings within a courtyard, the number of rooms denoting wealth and status. None but royalty were allowed to have 100 rooms, so nobles had to make do with 99.

As a living village, there are real market gardeners, potters, mulberry paper makers, blacksmiths, spinners and weavers, demonstrating their crafts. Under an awning of the village restaurant you can sample a Korean meal from steaming vats of noodles, but care is needed with the spicy sauces and the fiery *kimchi*. This revolting concoction of pickled and fermented cabbage is an addiction with Koreans, but will blow most European heads off. Vast quantities are made every autumn and stored in huge stoneware jars. It can be seen (and smelt) in every market.

On the steps of the Provincial Governor's Palace, actors portray the well-nourished and stately official and some of his retinue of women. This demonstrates the national costume of silk gowns with a high bodice, falling in many folds to the ground, with contrasting muffs two feet long, showing that the lady has no need to do housework.

Two or three times a day, there is a demonstration of folk dances, ranging from the graceful fan dance, more or less standardised from Hong Kong to Tokyo, Peking, Taiwan, Kuala Lumpur and Bangkok; and the athletic farmers' dance. This is a vigorous display of speed and agility: some 20 men twirling around the arena in formation or individually at high speed, beating a changing rhythm, while flicking 20ft-long ribbons from their hats.

Another short trip is to the tomb of the last King of the Yi dynasty, King Sunjong, who ruled from 1907 to 1910, and died only in 1926. Like most royal tombs, his is a tumuli mound, with an avenue of marble figures representing civil and military officials and various animals mounting guard. This seems to be a copy of the Ming Tombs in China. The setting amidst pinewoods made a pleasant venue for a class of schoolchildren who no doubt enjoyed combining a history lesson with a picnic. So did I.

Korea's other main seat of culture is Kyongju in the south-east, near the Japan Sea. There are expressways with good bus services, but for once I chose the newly-opened express train, with reclining seats in air-conditioned carriages, which covers the 260 miles in four and a half hours. The countryside was lovely. The forested hills were touched with accents of scarlet maples and golden gingko trees. The paddy harvest was in full swing; fields turned russet, with the hand-cut sheaves laid flat in neat patterns to dry, or stacked upright in long low walls. Because the modern high-yield rice has to be threshed *in situ*, there were portable threshers driven by small motors in many fields.

Todaiji Temple housing the bronze Daibutsu Buddha cast in
749 A.D. Biggest wooden building in the world

Entrance Kiyo Mizu Temple, Kyoto

Amida Buddha, Kamakura

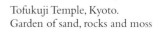

Tofukuji Temple, Kyoto.
Garden of sand, rocks and moss

A Rissaldar of the President's bodyguard, Delhi

Rissaldars of the President's bodyguard, Delhi.
All are parachutists and over 6 feet

The bath, Udaipur

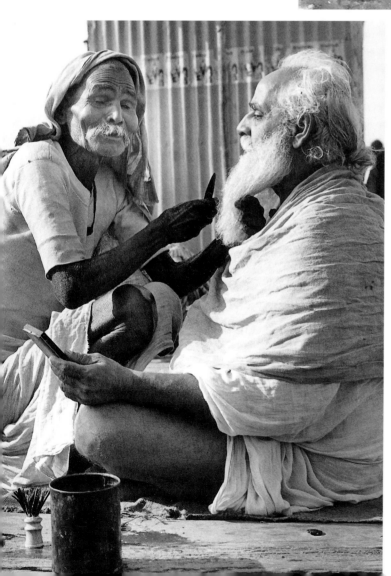

Pilgrim Trim. A spruce-up before a dip in the
Ganges at Benares (Varanasi today)

Fort Frederick, Trincomalee, Ceylon. Built by
the Dutch 1675. Father's first posting

The G.P.O. Calcutta with sacred guests

Queen Victoria by Sir George Frampton, R.A. Calcutta

Dalhousie Square. The long low building is the writers' offices of the East India Company. 1780

Armistice day ceremony, Hong Kong 11 November 1971. The 100 year old club behind and the cricket club on right are now replaced by skyscrapers

English Church on the Mall, Simla

Aberdeen harbour, Hong Kong. 20,000 boat people live on Sampans in 1971

Mother Teresa with abandoned babies, Calcutta

St. Paul's School Chapel, Mount Kanchenjunga behind

Darjeeling Hill Railway

Mount Kanchenjunga 45 miles from Darjeeling

A Tibetan beggar

Tibetan girls

Tibetan woman turning prayer wheels

Tamil tea pickers, Silent Valley estate, Munnar

Guderale Tea Estate. Showing factory and workers' lines

Tamil wedding, Munnar

The Drummer

Carrying her lunch to work on a tea estate, Kanan Devan Hills

Hanging up your hat is a tradition on retirement at
High Range Club, Munnar, 1967

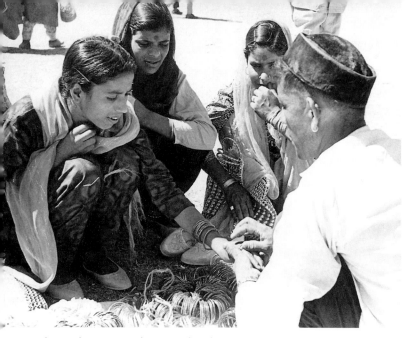

Bangle merchant at Dussehra Festival, Kulu

Brass-headed village God brought to festival

Winter migration. Flocks descend Beas valley from Ladakh

Silver trumpets, Manali

Revolving swings at Dussehra Festival, Kulu

Woman's work, Kulu

A stylish couple of Karonese
Bataks, Lingga, Sumatra
(A tribe once cannibal)

A hat for Ascot?

Mission church above paddy fields, Samosir island in lake Toba, Sumatra

The chief's house with
stone tables and chairs,
Ambarita

Royal council house of
former King of the
Simalungun Bataks,
Pematang Purba

Preparing rice seedlings, Bogor, Java

Drying paddy on the road, Bandung

Sunrise at 7600 ft Mount Bromo, Java. The crater drops on right

Borodudur. One of 72 Buddhas on the top circular terrace

The Buddha preaching, low relief at Borodudur

Hanging graves, Lemo, A Toraja village

Palawa village

Toraja headman's house, Palawa village. The
buffalo horns denote many funeral feasts

Carrying home the toddy brewed from palm sap
which can be seen foaming in the bamboo tubes,
Rantepao

Torajas waiting for the bus after working in paddy fields

A Pinisi, trading schooner of Buginese sailors,
formerly noted for piracy. Built at Ujung
Pandang, the shape of the bowsprit copies Toraja
house design

Angkor Wat over the inner moat

Battle in a jungle between Khmers and Chams. The Bayon

The commander in Chief directs the battle from an elephant. The Bayon

Lonely sentry at a ruin. Ta Prom

royal terrace, Angkor

ntrance to the Bayon

he Bayon. The balustrade represents a naga (snake) hauled by
pposing giants and demons to churn the sea of milk to produce
nrita (nirvana) a Hindu concept

Strangled, Angkor Wat

The Bayon. 49 such towers portray Jayavarman VII

Pas de deux. Apsaras
dance on a lotus,
The Bayon

Royal Apsaras, Angkor
Wat

The Corps de Ballet,
Angkor Wat

Mother's help. Siem Reap, Cambodia

Making whoopee, The Bayon

Daily chore for daughter, water comes
from Sra Srang Lake, created by the
builders of Angkor Wat

Chinthe and Pagoda,
Mandalay hill

Shwedagon Pagoda,
Rangoon

Worshippers at a shrine, Shwedagon Pagoda

Leg Rower,
Lake Inle

Cigar smoking woman,
Pagan

Pulguksa Temple, Kyongju

Buddha Altar, Pulguksa Temple

Guardians of the tomb of King Sunjong, last of the Chosun dynasty who died in 1926

A Bhikku, Pulguksa Temple

Hong Yurang Tomb. Officials and animal guardians

A new tourist development at Bomun Lake, just outside Kyongju, designed around an artificial reservoir, overlooks tennis courts, a golf course, boating marina and distant hills. There is a shopping arcade and all buildings are in traditional Korean style, with tiled roofs. Roads are lined with gingko, magnolia, acer and pine trees, clipped azaleas, marigolds and chrysanthemums, and so well tended that dead leaves are swept up almost as soon as they fall.

In Tumuli Park, the graves of Silla Kings are clustered under massive grassy mounds, some of which have been excavated, and their treasures displayed in a museum. The Flying Horse tomb has been opened up to show how the royal burial took place. The wooden coffin with its jewel gifts was covered by 15ft of boulders, then another 20ft of earth. Archaeologists have unearthed superb golden crowns, green glazed pottery and original paintings; diggings continue.

To reach the most holy Sokkuram Shrine on a hill above Pulguksa Temple involved driving through woods on a road with 99 curves, and then a ten-minute walk. The famous statue of Buddha was carved in AD 752 as an offering to enlist divine help against the Japanese, who always coveted Korea as an overflow space for their overcrowded island.

Pulguksa is one of the oldest monasteries in Korea, having been first built in AD 535, and many times reconstructed. In its latest form it is a huge building, based on large squared stones, loosely piled up, and with long terraces surmounted by tiled roofs with most elaborate painted wooden decoration under the eaves. There are many smaller pavilions, all with the same insistence on the eaves as the focal point. Their interiors are brightly decorated with painted walls and statues of Buddha. The three main pavilions have three different Buddhas, for there are of course different schools of Buddhism, just as there are with Christianity. Sometimes Avalhitesvara, the Boddhisattva of mercy, otherwise known as Kuan-Yin, is shown. A Boddhisattva is one who has attained the understanding of Nirvana but has elected not to profit from that personally, but to remain in this world to help others reach understanding.

Perhaps to help me reach understanding, I was shown round by Park Seo Inh, an English-speaking monk who was a Colonel in the US Marine Corps, and has been to the USA. He has now entered the austere regime of monkhood, renouncing all family connections. If you travel long enough in Asia you are bound to come across such cases. I have known many. Once in a luxury hotel in Delhi it was the wife and very beautiful model daughter that I met. Yes, she said, my husband has 'gone to God', but he sees us now and again. He was, by coincidence, also a Colonel, in the Indian Army.

An expressway leads from Kyongju to Pusan, the great port city of 3 million people and a prime shipbuilding centre, on the south-eastern corner of Korea. Here were crowds of holidaymakers on the curving Haeundae Beach, and there was time to visit the United Nations Cemetery (which marks the cost of the Korean war with 2,277 graves, of which 884 are from Britain) before flying back to Seoul.

A farewell dinner and floor show at a hotel out in the country rivalled anything Las Vegas can put on, because a large part of it was traditional Korean folklore, including a marriage celebration with villagers in a teahouse, and a deafening demonstration of Korean drumming: 20 huge drums suspended on a platform above the tables and reflected in a mirror on the stage.

22

The Truth about Bali

In Bali I saw the only happy large community I have seen in my life.
Geoffrey Gorer, *Bali and Angkor*

A letter of introduction from Apa Pant, the Indian High Commissioner in London, to the Chakorde of Ubud, the Village of Art in Bali, led in turn to an invitation to the wedding of the Chakorde's nephew. And what a red letter day that was! It encompassed three of the traditional ceremonies of Bali: a wedding, a cremation and a teeth-filing.

Incantations and purification ceremonies started in the morning with ritual blessings by a white-clad priest. The village was *en fête* with elaborate decorations which only the Balinese know how to fashion from simple and natural objects: carved palm and banana leaves, strips of bamboo twisted into patterns, mountains of fruit on silver dishes, sculptures of pork fat and dyed rice-cakes, and flowers, flowers everywhere. The women were gorgeous, in multi-coloured saris of silk, in batik patterns, surmounted by tight-fitting blouses and narrow-waisted jackets, flowers in the hair, the *salwar-kameez* which makes the best of any girl.

The final ceremony in the evening took place in a tented pavilion, also much decorated, where the relatives gathered closely around a low stage where the bride and groom sat before the priest, now bedizened in necklaces and a scarlet cap. It was a privilege to be allowed to get a close-up of the ceremony.

The teeth-filing did not involve the young couple, but a middle-aged lady, perhaps an aunt. She wore the most gorgeous outfit, and was borne on the shoulders of two men into the pavilion. Once again I was witness to the 'decisive moment' when the priest's little file was inserted into the mouth of the unfortunate lady, held securely by her relatives to endure what must have been literally a 'teeth shuddering' experience. Ensuring a straight alignment of the teeth is considered a mark of culture among the upper classes in Bali. In some other parts of the world, it is more elegant to have them filed into points. The thought of either sets my (few) teeth on edge. Stranger than

105

either is the fashion for aristocratic ladies of Japan during my grandfather's sojourn there at the time of the Meiji Restoration, to have their teeth painted black.

During a break in the marriage ceremonies, there was a funeral (unconnected) of a Brahmin priest. A coffin in Bali is always an animal, usually a lion or a bull. For this priest his bull had been under construction in the village for a week: a full-size animal with all its natural functions in working order, and of course in white, the sacred colour. It was borne on the shoulders of about 25 men, who cavorted boisterously along the street, turning it round, shaking it, pausing at any stream to douse it with water; all designed to confuse any evil spirits from following. The bull did not contain the priest's body at this stage. As we made our way, in the extreme heat of midday, for about a mile to a clearing in the forest, we were followed by a pagoda 30ft high, constructed like the bull from a timber frame, covered in papier-mâché, painted and decorated with all the elaborate fantasies of Balinese invention. This contained the body. Streaming from it were two long white strips representing the priest's spirit, which were held by the relatives. Only after arrival at the cremation ground was the body transferred to the bull, now placed on the funeral pyre of logs, and as the flames took hold, the beautiful pagoda was dismantled and fed to the fire.

A funeral is not regarded as a tragedy (unless of course it is caused by an accident), but as a celebration because in the Hindu world of Bali there is a certainty of rebirth – be it in a higher or a lower status, or even as an animal. So death is a natural release from earthly bonds; as also for the Buddhists who believe that it is the nature of all things to change, until the ultimate realisation of Nirvana – which for most people is never. What is Nirvana? That is a question like the Zen *koan*: 'What is the sound of one hand clapping?'

To say that Bali is one's favourite spot is to invite the retort that 'Bali is old hat; ruined by hordes of package tourists'. True up to a point; the Jumbo charter jets, especially from Germany, descend on Denpasar with monotonous regularity. Traffic pollutes, hotels proliferate, but there is still a law that no hotel may be built higher than the palm trees. Cynics proclaim that the ethnic dances are only done for the tourists. Not true. The dancers are farmers and fishermen, and if they accept tourist dollars in their spare time, that is perfectly natural. Moreover, a percentage of their earnings goes to the village *bandjar* or cooperative to help with their temple festivals. Travel to the inland villages and watch a local performance of the Barong or the Ketchak, and see how the people love it, note the reactions of the children to the conflict between the Barong and Rangda the Witch, or how they understand every turn in the Ramayana story of the abduction of Sita by Ravana and her rescue by Rama with the aid of the monkey armies of Hanuman.

Bali is different. The Hinduism of Bali is different from India's. Though caste rules apply, all except priests may eat beef. The cow is not sacred. In addition to the Hindu pantheon of gods, a host of spirits are worshipped: the

106

spirits of mountain, stream, tree, house, which must be propitiated by the right ceremonies. Watch the housewife leave the handful of rice or a flower on her doorstep. See the processions of women bearing works of art on their heads, to celebrate their temple's festival day. When Mount Gunung Agung erupted in 1963 and flowed down to the sea at Sanur Beach, causing much loss of life, it was because the proper ceremonies had not been offered.

The Indian Chola Dynasty, the people who built that lovely little Shore Temple and the rock carvings associated with it at Mahabalipuram in the seventh century, were colonialists, expanding their empire to Sumatra and Java. In due course, when the proselytising arm of Islam took over, many of the high castes, Brahmins and Kshatriyas, disliked the harsh discipline of the Sword of Islam, and took refuge in Bali. The Muslims, for some reason, did not follow. Thus came about Bali's isolation as an island of Hinduism with a leavening of Buddhism, already present in Java.

When Dutch colonialism imposed its system of forced agriculture, they did not at first bother about developing Bali. Not until 1906 did they tackle the problem of the seven small states (ruled by independent Sultans) in the usual colonial way – with guns. Here they had a shock, for they found that when confronted with overwhelming force, the Balinese Princes did not surrender, nor run away, but with their entire courts, put on their finest clothes and jewellery, and marched out to die under the Dutch machine guns. This was the *Puputan*, identical to the *Jauhar* of the Rajputs in India. Honour is preserved, and the enemy is shamed – as the Dutch were. The shock, in this day and age, within our lifetime, can be imagined. Not surprisingly, a people who can do this also practise *Sati* (or *Suttee*): the immolation of wives on the funeral pyre of their husbands. The practice continues today occasionally, as in India.

So what sort of people are the Balinese? Ethnically the people of Indonesia belong to the Malay race – though east of the Wallace Line which falls between Bali and Lombok you start to find Melanesian influences. A Malay characteristic is to 'run *Amok*': a Malay word. And there must be an element of *amok* in the *Puputan*. This was seen in a political sense in the chaotic post-war times when the Dutch strove to reassert their empire. When one of the leaders of the independence struggle, Ngurah Rai was defeated, there was a *Puputan* of 150 of his followers in 1946. Later still, when Sukarno's leadership of independent Indonesia was threatened by the communists, there was a pogrom, in Bali alone, which claimed the lives of somewhere between 70,000 and 100,000 people (the true figures will never be known). This, if you please, was 1966!

Heavens above, this was only four years before my first visit in 1970! And I thought I was in Paradise! I said Bali is different. As a balletophile, brought up on Colonel de Basil's Ballets Russes de Monte Carlo, I found myself in a wonderland of dance. Ignorant of Bali's history, I revelled in the seductive sounds of the gamelan orchestra that greeted me every time I entered the air-conditioned solace of the Bali Beach Hotel on Sanur Beach, and succumbed to the charms of the Balinese female figure – for surely no breasts can be more tautly up-pointed, no skins more smooth and voluptuous, no hair more finely combed and set, no clothes more gracefully worn, no control of eyes, lips, fingers, legs, torso, more precise than those of the girls who are trained from age 5 to perform the most graceful and expressive of all dances.

23

A River in Chinese Time

China? There lies a sleeping giant. Let him sleep, for when he wakens, he will move the world.

Napoleon (attributed)

It was late in 1978 that the thaw started in China, and Mao began to echo Lenin's cry of 1921, 'Enrich yourselves' signalling a weakening (temporarily) in the rigid concepts of communism. So we felt ourselves like pioneers when a party of 23 package tourists, plus courier, broached communist China in April 1979.

Flying on a Pakistan Airlines Jumbo to Rawalpindi, where I had been touring only a month before, and changing to a Boeing 707, we flew over the snowy wilderness of the Karakorams and across the vast belly of China to Peking. We found China already well prepared for foreign tourism, though there were echoes of their brothers-in-arms, the Russian communists who had only recently deserted the country, leaving mementoes by way of old-fashioned hotels. But who's complaining? They fed us well everywhere, and were painfully anxious to please. As for the Chinese citizens, they found their western guests such a novelty, such a weird spectacle, that they lined up to goggle at us.

This was evident from the first excursion laid on, which was naturally to the Great Wall: nothing could be more Chinese or more typical. Our departure from the railway station was witnessed by a large crowd which had been well marshalled into two wedges, leaving a wide avenue for us to enter. We felt like celebrities, uncertain whether to bow, so we compromised with comradely waves. Unfortunately the thaw had not yet extended to styles of dress; everybody was still buttoned up to the neck in the drab military tunics of black or blue. They had only recently been told to put away their 'Little Red Books' of Mao's sayings, which they used to wave in the face of all and sundry. It was the rarest thing to see a girl in a coloured frock. How different now, when the Chinese dress as variously and as smartly as anywhere else. At the Wall, the crowds were so great that our notoriety was submerged in the mass, for the Chinese are great travellers too.

What can one say about the Wall, except that it is there, so large, so old, so long that it can be seen from the Moon? Well, if you must know, it is 6,350kms long, though only 2,300kms direct from one end to the other. It was first built in the sixth century BC, but rebuilt in the Ming Dynasty, about 1560. It is 7m high, 6m wide at the base, and 5m wide at the top. Like Hadrian's Wall, built to restrain the savage Scots, the Chinese wanted their wall wide enough for a troop of horsemen to gallop to danger points. However, they would have had great difficulty in doing this in several sections that we tackled, where the staircases are so steep that it is scarcely possible to climb up without using the handrails and chains provided. There are 25,000 towers, from which warnings of approaching enemies could be made by smoke (day) and fires (night). Cannon shots signalled the number of enemies.

We had a somewhat similar feeling, of being confronted by something so vast, so complicated that it cannot be comprehended, when we passed through the Gate of Heavenly Peace under Mao's smiling face, to enter the Forbidden City. Acres of carved white marble, courtyard leading to court-yard, terraces bounded by railings of carved marble pillars, staircases of which the centre section is a slope filled with writhing dragons on which only the Son of Heaven may tread. Through the Gate of Heavenly Purity we reached the Hall of Supreme Harmony – or is it the other way round? Bronze and gilt dragons, with the five claws which only Imperial Dragons may have, tortoises and storks, emblems of long life and faithfulness, welcomed us as we penetrated deeper into the most august buildings until we reached the Throne Room with its cover of Imperial Yellow silk, last occupied by the ruthless and long-lived Empress Tzu Shi, and her ineffectual son Pu Yi, who became a puppet of the Japanese invaders, installed as Emperor of Manchuria, and finally a humble gardener in the slums of democratic Peking.

Then to the Temple of Heaven, in a peach orchard in blossom, where the Emperor prays annually for a blessing on his people's crops, and plants a symbolic sowing of rice. Then to the Summer Palace which overlooks a lake where boats are rowed as if it were the Serpentine. Moon Bridges are built so steeply arched that they form a semicircle: and thus the reflection completes a 'moon'. A huge boat of stone, alleged to have been built by the Empress with money required for her navy, is named the 'Marble Boat of Quiet Banquets'. The Navy went short so that the Empress could have her banquets – quietly.

The high point of our journey was to be a cruise on the Yangtze, through the four famous gorges, which are now being flooded as a result of the giant dams which will control the devastating floods which have been the curse of the Yangtze. In the great flood of 1931, 140,000 people were drowned and 12 million made homeless. The 70,000 square miles flooded were equal to the area of England and most of Scotland. The river, which is 3,964 miles long, rises in Tibet and flows into the Pacific at Shanghai. It is so big that it is tidal for 239 miles from the sea. Clearly a problem for China, and it is being tackled in the boldest possible way; a giant dam to tame the giant river. Work started in 1994, and already the first effective dam and lock has sealed off the ancient stream. But it is such a gigantic undertaking – submerging the gorges which extend for 140 miles, destroying thousands of villages and uprooting millions of people, creating a lake hundreds of miles long, which will eventually silt up and raise the water level again – that there are grave doubts about the whole scheme. Indeed, there are strong objections, but the mighty force has been set in motion.

To start our river cruise, we flew to Chungking, the wartime capital where Chiang Kai Shek's army held out against the invading Japanese. Military supplies were ferried to Chungking by road from northern Burma, and by air from Assam in eastern India; American and RAF pilots flying 'over the hump' – a flight made perilous by high mountains and bad weather.

Chungking is not a pretty place – or was not when we saw it. Straggling over steep hills with stairways winding up from the river, it is a great commercial port, though the loading and unloading of goods is of the most primitive kind, carried out by coolie labour. The city was badly damaged by bombing in the war, but I sensed a fine spirit of 'can do', exemplified by a museum, an art college, and a kindergarten where the little moppets, all rouged and lipsticked and tutued, pranced and posed in *tableaux vivants*. Our hotel was converted from the Peoples' Hall, a big circular domed theatre with two wings added for the hotel; red pillars and blue-tiled roofs, all spick and span. For bedrooms we had high-ceilinged suites – comprising a sitting room with desk, a bedroom and a bathroom with a huge tiled bath. Lavish towels and fine blankets and quilts were provided, though it was 80°F in the room. Presumably we were tasting the fruits of an *aparatchick*'s perks. A dinner at another hotel was a banquet, course after course; somebody counted 27. It seemed they couldn't do enough to show us how well off China is; but wasn't it just the same in pre-war Russia?

As in Peking, we were like freak shows as we toured the markets, watching eels being skinned, ourselves surrounded by gaping crowds. One very pretty girl in crimson blouse kept shying away from my camera, but her curiosity compelled her to keep returning, until I eventually got a shot of her through the coach windscreen, to the amused delight of the crowd.

Driving to the embarkation pier for our 727-mile cruise down-river to Wuhan, which would take three days and nights, we passed a long queue of military trucks and tanks, waiting to cross the river by primitive ferries. They were destined for Vietnam. Our ship, a four-decker of about the size of a pre-war Channel ferry, was strictly divided into two classes. The lower deck, open-sided, was packed with the poorer classes and their chattels, camping in the corridors. Higher up were cabins, and on the top deck, saloons fore and aft. When we took our meals in the aft saloon, strictly first class, inquisitive noses were pressed to the windows. Cabins, four-berth and two-berth, were inside and outside. I was in one of four grim iron berths, sharing a washbasin in which the water ran brown. There was one bath, and one WC (dry but clean). The bath was for ladies only. We survived, and the food, as usual, was quite good.

The river, before Wan Hsien, where we had a shore visit and were entertained by the City Revolutionary Committee, was highly industrial. Factories poured out black smoke from the banks, and discharged evil-looking chemical compounds into the water. Nature conservation has little place in China as yet. Approaching the three groups of gorges, which extend for 140 miles, the river traffic was a never-ending source of interest, everything from steamers, tugs towing or pushing heavy barges, and countless *sampans*, sailed or rowed, in which the age-old commerce of China proceeds. Some craft had a single fisherman; others had 16 rowers. There were vicious whirlpools, and as we reached the gorges, they narrowed in one place to no more than the Corinth Canal; but with the difference that their sides towered up with jagged projections for thousands of feet. Here I suffered the most grievous fate that a photographer can – the weather turned grim, dark and raining, so unless one wanted to convey an impressionistic landscape of the Styx, it was a dead loss. The mountain peaks were hidden in the clouds.

One thing that remained clearly visible to the eye, if not to the camera, was the pathway, cut out of the banks and even from the sheer rock of the gorges, for the tugmen, the human tugs or hauliers, upon whose backs rested all upstream navigation of the river. In squads of 500 or more, with lines attached to the masts of *sampans*, they hauled away from morning to night, feeding and resting for the night where they lay, in fine weather or foul. Their story, if ever it were told, must surely be an extreme example of human misery.

And the future, after the dams are completed, what does it hold? The devastating floods downstream may, or may not, be cured, for it is not just the Yangtze that is responsible. There are seven tributaries whose water – and sewage – all contribute. The river will rise hundreds of feet, wiping out thousands of towns; the gorges will become wider. Navigation will continue, as it must, through locks, which are already in use. One thing is sure: nobody will ever again be able to see them as we did, 20 years ago.

For further information (as they say, but I am not selling the reader anything), consult Simon Winchester's 1997 book, *River at the Centre of the World: A Journey up the Yangtse and Back, in Chinese Time.*

A farewell dinner in Peking, at the 100-year-old Tung Lei Shun restaurant, revealed the secret of cooking Peking Duck. Start with the specially bred white Peking duck. Blow air under its skin to distend it and make it crisp. Fill the body with water and suspend it over a hot fire of aromatic wood, basting for a long time with molasses First eat the crisp skin. Then eat the meat in a thin pancake with spring onions, dipped in rich sweet soya sauce. Finish with soup from the duck's bones.

24

Far-Flung Fiji

When I hit the Southern hemisphere, my mental map was disoriented, because the sun always seemed to be in the 'wrong' place. To spend a fortnight in Australia and another in New Zealand is to take a very small bite out of two very big apples. So why not take a nibble out of a rather smaller island which is not far away – as distances go in the Pacific, where 10,000 miles is only just over the horizon.

Bula: as I was greeted by everyone in Fiji, surely one of the friendliest of places. And why not, since they welcomed Queen Victoria as their Queen, and though political differences caused them to withdraw from the Commonwealth for a few years, they are snugly back in again. In any case, they drive on the left, they play cricket and rugby – and what rugby! For Fijians are notably large, heavy, and famed for their beef and brawn.

The only unfamiliar touch concerns the uniforms of their Police Force, and their Army (at least its ceremonial band). In each case the uniform is designed to suit the hot and humid tropical climate. Beneath a normal jacket of blue, both wear white skirts, with scalloped edges, white for the police, pink for the army. Nothing could be smarter than their drill, as I saw when they piped a band to see off a cruise liner from Suva.

Fiji is about the size of Hawaii or Wales and consists of two main islands and a host of smaller ones. Among these is the island of Beqa, pronounced Mbengga whose people are noted for their fire-walking powers – no tricks, just faith; a genuine miracle. *Copra* (the meat of the coconut) and sugar cane are the main crops, and it is sugar that is Fiji's problem. Not the growing of it; it grows 'like a weed', but the cutting of it. This is a hot, dusty and unpleasant job, and the Fijians don't care for it. The solution was clear to our Victorian politicians: in India there were millions of unemployed, longing for a steady job and accustomed to the discomforts of tropical agriculture. So, they were shipped to Fiji in their thousands, and being hard-working and also more prolific than the Fijians, they soon became more prosperous. Had matters been left alone they would soon have become the majority and would eventually have bought up and controlled most of the islands. So measures were taken, early on, to deny the Indians, who were only indentured labourers, the right to own land. They may only lease it. This gave rise to friction, and in recent years to riots and a military revolution, resulting in the temporary withdrawal of Fiji from the Commonwealth.

The reality of the difference between the races was made very clear to me when chatting to a taxi driver on a small island. He only earned $11 a week, he said, but this was enough because he grew all his own food, and had a small patch of sugar cane too. With an inherited home, surrounded by coconuts, bananas, jack fruit, durians, paw-paw ... who would want to work harder? Well, Indians would. As a laid-back paradise, Fiji has few equals. The Indians are still the richest, owning most of the businesses.

Fiji's international airport, Nadi (pronounced Nandi) lies at the opposite end of the main island to the capital, Suva; and somewhere in between I found my 'desert island hideaway' with all mod cons – one of many modern hotels springing up around Pacific Harbour. Actually I *can* say it is a desert island, for it is on Yanuca Island, reached by a bridge. The long white beach was deserted as the sun sank below the palms, and I sank into a long chair with my sundowner and thoughts of Somerset Maugham.

An excellent dinner under the palms, and we were regaled with a *meke*, the traditional Fijian welcome of song and dance. The men were wearing the grass skirts while the women were demurely dressed in long white skirts. Pity. However, the men carried spears and did war dances, beating time by banging their spears on the floor. The women's dances involved no great physical effort for they were performed with the hands while sitting down. They ended with the Fijian farewell, *Isa Lei*. I swear it is the most haunting, tear-jerking melody in the world.

Blue Lagoon Cruises offered a short cruise by yacht through the Yasawa Islands, specks of sparsely inhabited coconut plantations encircled by lagoons and necklaces of coral. About as far away from western civilisation as one could wish. The *Lycianda* was a trim little motor ship of 227 tons, carrying 40 passengers in 20 air-conditioned cabins, each with private shower and toilet. (Discomfort I can endure when necessary, but I will never volunteer for it.) There were no frills; the cabin's walls were the ship's steel sides. No saloon either; a long table on the awning-covered afterdeck served for meals and lounging. Passengers were an international crowd: Americans, Australians, New Zealanders, Germans, Danes, Belgians. In case of bad weather, side curtains could enclose the deck, but for us the sun shone on our South Seas adventure.

Setting course from Lautoka north-west into the wide Pacific, the wind brought welcome relief from the heat. Cruising close along the coral reefs and inside lagoons, we anchored 50 yards offshore at Nanuya Lailai on a beach of whitest sand fringed with coconut palms. Only five families lived on the island, about 20 people in all; with yams, taro, paw-paw, tapioca and fishing to support them. Their only trade was in *copra* from the coconuts, and

114

making baskets, or selling seashells to occasional tourists. I tried to imagine life where travel anywhere from your home means the ocean. Not surprisingly, islanders of the Pacific are all skilled sailors. Our Fijian crew swam ashore to secure our bows to a palm tree, then snorkled to shoot fish. Our Captain, Leka Tuiqereqere (Anglicised to Leonard) came from this island; an example of enterprise. He went to New Zealand to work as a sailor, studied navigation in his spare time for his Master's Certificate, and was a thoroughly modern citizen of the world. His father and grandfather were also sailors.

Michael, the Chief Engineer, belonged to the fire-walking tribe of Beqa Island. Leonard told a good story of a dwarf found in an eel-bed who was the God of Fire, and conferred immunity from pain when fire-walking on this tribe, in return for being spared when caught by a man who had sinned and was sent to catch eels as a penance. It was a slightly mixed up yarn; but there is no doubt the men from that island are genuine fire-walkers with a unique ability to suffer no harm.

On one island we were duly introduced to the *Kava* ceremony; its preparation by steeping the roots of the pepper plant in water, fermentation assisted (by tradition if hopefully not in our case) by copious spitting by the women who squeeze the juices out. As a ceremony, it bears comparison with the Japanese tea ceremony.

Our most memorable dinner was cooked in a *lovo* oven on the beach. Joints of beef and pork, with yams, taro and tapioca were wrapped in banana leaves and laid on heated stones at the bottom of a pit and covered with sand. After five or six hours this produced the most delicious meal I can remember; savoured all the more because we sat on benches, with bottles of wine, illuminated by flaring torches and a brilliant full moon shining through the palm tops.

At another, larger island, Nacula, about 30 people had walked from villages several miles away to set up a market on the beach where we landed, selling shells, bead necklaces and woven baskets. At yet another island, Sawa-i-Lau, it was very different; a rocky peak of 1,000ft, honeycombed with caves and small holes where trees grew. No soil was visible. In a large blow-hole of a cave, we climbed over rocks to find an inner cavern, where several of the crew made spectacular high dives.

Nabukeru was a larger island with a beautifully-kept village showing communal planning. The scent of a frangipani enveloped the widely-spaced houses, kitchens separate and toilets dispersed on the outskirts. The village provides a house for a newly-married couple. A tin-roofed Methodist chapel was white and airy inside.

Some quite mountainous islands then hove in sight. Waya, an island about eight miles long, rises to 2,000ft, and has 4,000 inhabitants. Meeting the Headmaster of the school, he told us he had seven teachers and 240 pupils, some of whom walked several miles to school. All teaching is in English and starts at age 6. The football field is for rugby, and portraits of the Queen and Prince Philip were on the walls.

At one island, enterprising villagers provided a *Meke* to entertain us, and brought it on board! The initiative of a local noble, Ratu Epeli, had organised a group to keep alive traditional songs and dances, which involved beating a rhythm with sticks on the floor. Dressed in grass skirts, men and girls, they came aboard and gave of their best, ending with a dance in which all joined. I had no idea at the time, but it turned out that Ratu Epeli was the father of the then president of Fiji, Sir Penaia Epeli, who died in 1993. It was as if Mrs Thatcher's father had joined a group of Morris dancers.

I could never exhaust the pictorial or historic interest of Asia, but now it is time for another interval in the movie. The action transfers first to Europe, then via Madagascar to the Western Hemisphere.

Reel 5

Action Moves West

25

Land Without Women

The female of the species is more deadly than the male.

Kipling

If a misogynist really wants to retire from the world and be free from all feminine influences in the form of women, cows or bitches, there is always Mount Athos. But you can't just walk in there and ask for a room. Oh no. Casual visitors are not welcome. You are supposed to have a nobler motive than mere curiosity; and to be, if not a religious pilgrim, then at least someone (a man of course) with a genuine intellectual interest in the monastic way of life. Journalists do not qualify as such; but my intellectual interest was genuine enough. After all, I've been a student of all religions all my life, starting with a very firm grounding in Victorian Christianity, and have illustrated many books and encyclopedias on the religions of the world.

Negotiations for a permit started in London and continued through the Greek Foreign Ministry and our Consulate in Salonika. It is difficult to remember now who I prevailed upon to vouch for my respectability; but in the end it seemed pretty much of a formality to satisfy our Consul, and the permit was duly issued for a stay of two nights.

The holy mountain of Athos is a rugged and mountainous promontory 40 miles long, the northernmost of the three fingers of Halkidiki peninsula which projects into the Aegean from northern Greece. It has been for 1,000 years an independent state with a monastic civil government of the Orthodox Church, which broke away from Rome in 1054. There are about 20 monasteries and some 2,000 monks. Some monasteries, such as Lavra, are huge and very rich; others are decrepit and very poor. All have some priceless treasures of ecclesiastical art. For centuries Mount Athos has been one of the most tempting sites for researchers and art historians, but access is strictly controlled. For non-Greeks, visitors are limited to ten per year, so I must consider myself lucky to have been one of the ten in 1973.

Approaching via Salonika (Thessaloniki) gave a pre-taste of Byzantine churches and art. Salonika was founded in 315 BC by Cassander, one of

119

Alexander's generals. Behind the city the ancient fortified walls rise to an Acropolis, surrounded by cobbled streets and houses with projecting balconies, a relic of nearly 500 years of Turkish occupation, which only ended in 1912. Alexander was born at Pella, a few miles to the west, and realistic mosaics, one showing Alexander on a lion hunt, were discovered in 1951. Aristotle, his teacher, was born at Stageira, near the Halkidiki coast, so there are many historical associations with a city which has seen the clash of Roman Legions, Persian and Greek Armies and Navies. Xerxes had a canal cut through the eastern finger, to avoid the stormy isthmus of Mount Athos, but no trace of it remains.

Mount Athos is often thought of as an island, for there is no land access to its 6,000ft peak. An ocean voyage is necessary, from the small port of Ouranopolis, in a caique which chugs along the coast for an hour or so, passing several monasteries, to deposit visitors at the tiny harbour and village of Daphni. Greek police accompany the caique to ensure that no women are smuggled ashore. Feminists need not apply. The edict of 1061 forbade entry to any female (animals included), any child, any eunuch, any smooth visage. Only in regard to this last is there relaxation; beards are no longer *de rigueur*.

Though the monasteries are obliged to offer a bed to all visitors, their catering is notoriously spartan, so it was a wise precaution to stock up with a good breakfast at Ouranopolis. Daphni was a bit chaotic; nobody spoke English or told us what to do. A few shops and a café under vines, police and customs posts; that was all. Permits and passports checked, it was indicated that we should take the decrepit bus which waited to take us up the mountain to the seat of local government, Karyes, where each monastery maintains a house and a representative to the Monastic Council. It took 50 minutes to grind up the rough tracks through sweet-smelling pine woods. A few bulls and stallions were grazing – on God knows what, for there were no fields, no cows or mares either! Karyes' red-brick domed church and stone houses make it quite a little town. At the monastic centre, our permits to stay were finally issued, and lay officials checked the day visitors for hair length. They refused entry to three young men; one Australian and two German.

It was very fortunate that one other English speaker was staying – Dimitri Rechkalov, an Australian from Sydney, son of a Cossack Colonel. The only means of transport is shank's pony, and as Lavra, the monastery best prepared for visitors, is five hours walk away, we decided on Koutloumoussi, which was only 15 minutes. We were received politely by an elderly monk who spoke Russian. He showed us the church with frescos round a corridor, and ikons and hanging brass lamps in the centre. There were two beautifully made reading tables inlaid with ivory and silver. Shown up to a sitting room with chairs around, we waited for the Abbot to call, but he never came. He must have been too busy, for they numbered only four in all. When almost dark, a very dirty old monk led us to a tiny kitchen where a table was set with two bowls of bean soup, two salads of herbs, and a minute piece of very salt fish roe in oil. We were hungry enough to enjoy it all, but the retsina wine was really undrinkable. The monk cautioned us not to go out on a wooden balcony: 'It's not safe,' he said, and judging from the wood, which looked as if it came from the coffin of a Pharaoh, he was probably right. We slept in a small room with three beds, each provided with a sheet and two blankets. The only ablutions were a tap over a sink green with slime. The toilets were holes in the floor, dropping the full four floors. We slept well, woken only once by bells; this was probably Matins, on the Byzantine clock at our 4 a.m. We were on the Julian calendar too.

I'm afraid we neglected our monastic duty by skipping Matins and rose at 6.30 a.m. As there was nobody about, we left the customary honorarium and cleared out. We tried to get breakfast at the so-called inn at Karyes, but there was no milk (of course) and no cheese; so we made do with lemon tea and dry bread. At least it was fresh; I photographed two laymen loading up a donkey with long loaves for delivery.

The bus was running, and took us down to Daphni to catch a boat for a ten-minute journey to Panteleimon, the big Russian monastery, where Dimitri would feel at home, and I was delighted to have someone who could translate. Panteleimon is built of many chapels and domes around the main church, painted red ochre with many onion domes and double crosses. To one side, overlooking the sea, is a huge five-storey building which was a pilgrimage centre, but was gutted by fire in 1960. Another even bigger building was the hospital. The way the whole ensemble towers up to the main dome is reminiscent of the Potala.

Dimitri had a letter of introduction, and we met the monks just coming out of·church. They were very welcoming, and invited us straight in to lunch. This was a feast compared to the previous day: tasty soup with round beans, bread, cheese, cold fish (*bacalhau*) in white sauce, rosé wine, and an orange. The big refectory was covered with frescos on the walls and ceiling.

The tower over the refectory has 24 bells, including an enormous two-ton one, made in Moscow in 1888; all were inexpertly played by Father Sergei at 8.30 p.m. With Dimitri's help, we had long conversations with some of the monks, of whom 15 remained in 1973. Father Serafin invited us to tea in his top-floor room, and gave us Nescafé and stale Easter cake. He had a gas stove in his room, used for baking communion bread, and kept sweets in sundry tins and jars on the shelves. Obviously a suspect binger (the monks are only allowed two meals a day).

Father Gavril, the Patriarch, gave us some figures on the population of his monastery: in 1914, 2,500. In 1930, 500. Now, 15. The Greek government was chary about admitting Soviet Russians during the period of the Cold War, and Father Avil was one of five who had been admitted in the 1960s; he was due to take over as Patriarch in due course.

It being Sunday, we attended a short service at 5.30 p.m., with much crossing and incense swinging. On the Monday there was a full service in the

121

main church with two priests in full golden vestments. The fat Father Docephy had a fine, strong intoning voice, and responses were made by an Albanian doorkeeper aged 84, who had been in the service of the monastery since age 11. In the Greek Orthodox Church, the *iconostassis* which blocks off the altar is a magnificent gilt screen, containing several ikons, and the priests move in and out from it.

26

Loopy about Lemurs

I love all animals, but I've been a bit loopy about lemurs ever since Johnny Morris used to come on *Animal Magic* feeding grapes to Dottie the ringtailed darling who perched on his shoulder. The only trouble is, they only live in Madagascar, which is such a long way away, at the bottom of the Indian Ocean where it was once, aeons ago, attached to Africa. So why didn't the lemurs spread? That's one for the biologists.

Enquiries showed that I could reach Antannanarivo, capital of Madagascar, on a flight via Paris, and that an internal flight would be needed to reach the southern reserve where the ringtails hang out. There were also the loud-mouthed Indris variety to be searched for in the jungle. There were no package tours, and it was beginning to look expensive. I hadn't the resources of Gerald Durrell who has done so much to save and popularise the lemurs; much less of John Cleese whom the BBC put through a jungle course, in return for which he made us laugh while enjoying the lemurs.

Studying maps and airlines revealed that a triangular flight plan could be set up between Madagascar, Mauritius and the French island of Réunion. With the cost of living, hotels and food, it was going to set me back a cool £2,000, and there wasn't a hope of seeing the money back; but at least it gave me the opportunity of three articles and a stock of pictures. And that is what I set out as my personal plot in the film of life – to travel where and when I want.

Antannanarivo, capital of Malagasy to give it the modern name, presents quite an obstacle course to the jet-lagged visitor after a three-stop, one change of airline flight of 24 hours. The socialist palaver over money indicates that they are very short of it, for all foreign money must be declared, listed and counted – by one man for the whole planeload. After which one is invited to step into one of six rabbit-hutches closed by white plastic curtains, where there is just room to stand beside a lady who merely wants to check your hand baggage. Then collect your passport and present it at another window before descending to ground level to reclaim luggage and present it to a second customs desk where every case is opened.

Tannanarivo (they usually leave off the first bit) is a very attractive town,

123

built round a lake encircled by deep blue jacarandas, overlooked by steep cliffs on which the Royal Palaces stand out like an Acropolis. Madagascar had a long line of Kings and Queens (mostly Queens as it happens), and with a slave society they were able to endow their palaces with Victorian luxury and indulge every whim, like being carried everywhere in a chair by slaves, since there were no roads. Queen Ranavalona the Cruel, who executed 100,000 of her subjects, was deposed by the French in 1897, when they abolished slavery. One of her dresses, a red velvet number from Worth of Paris, is on view in the Palace.

No less remarkable was her longest-lasting Prime Minister, Jean Laborde, a Frenchman who arrived, naked and shipwrecked in 1831. Being a mechanical genius, he made himself so useful that he introduced industry and modernised the country over 47 years. His portrait appears in the palace, and I noticed an extraordinary likeness to my taxi driver, who confirmed that he was a great-great grandson.

Lemurs are the trade-mark of Madagascar, but they were not very much in evidence. The zoo and botanical gardens had some in cages unfortunately, and others on three islands in a lake, where each family had a shelter and a tree to climb, and one could throw them bananas. The varieties were catta (ringtailed) shifaka (white) and kutrika (ruffed). Another animal unique to Madagascar, but now extinct, is the flightless bird, Aepyornis, whose legs were 8ft long, like a giant ostrich. Some of its bones are on view in the museum.

The trail of the ringtails leads one to the Reserve at Berenty, a short flight of 500 miles to Fort Dauphin in the extreme south. Sisal is the big industry here, and a Frenchman, M de Heaulme, manages a plantation and also the Lemur Reserve and the Hotel le Dauphin, with the best of French cuisine.

After the war Madagascar declared independence, but it has been a stony road. The French Army and Navy left in 1974; the government nationalised most European companies without compensation, so the semi-communist set-up naturally finds difficulty in obtaining European expertise. The birth rate is one of the highest in the world, and the population doubled in 15 years.

The hot and dry southern area has some of the most remarkable plants and trees in the world. It is a savage landscape of stony soil, from which grow the long green stems of *Didiera Procera* with tiny thorny leaves all the way up to 20ft culminating in a bunch of feathery flowers. It is surprising that the lemurs are able to jump and land on these without damaging their paws or feet. There are whole zarebas of prickly pear (*Opuntia*), pitcher plants (*Nepenthes*) which catch and digest insects which fall into their covered cups; and baobabs, whose smooth-skinned bulging trunks look like fat men sitting on the beach, waving their arms about at the top of the tree, like roots put on upside down.

The Antandroy tribe are very poor, raising cattle and making charcoal. Even their tribal Chief's house is a small wooden hut, with separate entrances for him and his chief wife. Seniority must be preserved; you can't have a woman coming in and out by the same door as her husband. Their funeral customs are strange too; bodies are dug up for a chat with their relatives after some years, dressed in fresh clothes and reburied. Memorials are carved from wood with due reference to the deceased's job in life, or how he died. One shows a little girl being eaten by a crocodile, a family paddling a boat, a housewife carrying a pail.

The lemurs, of which there are plenty in the forest of Berenty, proved elusive. They did not perform as they did for John Cleese, standing about waiting for titbits from Cleese and his crew, and jumping on and off the trees. They were semi-tame. On my visit, some years ago, they were still wild; sticking to the higher branches and making death-defying leaps from one tree to another, or to the uncomfortable-looking spiny thorns of *Didiera Procera*. They rarely descend to the ground, on which level they proceed with the most engaging gait – on their hind legs, arms and tail flying, leaping sideways.

Disappointing though it was to get no usable pictures of ringtails or shifakas, there was still another shot in my locker. Returning to Tannanarivo, and driving northward into a quite different sort of forest, a proper tropical rainforest, I sought the large Indris variety. With Domenica, a guide from the Ministry, in a Renault 4 which was so under-powered that we spent most of the time in third gear, we settled for a couple of nights at Andasibe, a station on the narrow-gauge line that runs to the coast. The Hotel Buffet de la Gare was what its name suggests: a large station buffet that caters for the daily train that stops there for 45 minutes to allow the passengers to lunch. As an after-thought, it has eight rooms offering modest and not too clean comfort. With the aid of a forest guard, we plunged into the Perinet Forest, hacking at dense undergrowth and hanging lianas with a machete, but in two days, early and late, we never saw an Indris, though we frequently heard their plaintive terri-torial calls above our heads.

Agriculture is so backward in Madagascar that in all the paddy fields we passed, there was not a single tractor or even a bullock to be seen. Men ploughed by hand with a narrow shovel, then stood knee-deep to smoothe out the mud, for planting out the seedlings by hand, as in Asia. By slash and burn economy, they have destroyed most of the forests, making matters worse; and of course the lemurs suffer, as do the orang-utans in Borneo.

Well, some you win; some you lose. I had two further calls to make. It was a little over two hours flight to Réunion, and as if by magic, I was in France. I knew that because I had landed in the middle of a strike. When my hired car was not ready, the lame explanation was that 'somebody has not done his job' – i.e. it's not *my* fault, monsieur. Even the doctors had declared a strike, except for emergencies.

Plenty of modern hotels and apartment blocks, a few European-style shops, a Chinese baker (Mr Ah Fah), an imposing Gendarmerie, and that was St Denis. Roads perfect, of course, with two 'flics' sitting on their motor bikes waiting to pounce on any infringement of the 110kph speed limit. What interested me most about Réunion was its central mountain which makes it a supreme health resort for the tropics. From the palm-fringed beaches I lost no time in driving up to Cilaos, where the road reaches 5,332ft in a crater which was obviously once a volcano. No wonder Frenchmen elect to do their national service in Réunion. I could spend a happy holiday there if I ever had time for a holiday.

It was only 25 minutes flight to Mauritius, and here I was in India. There was little to show that the island had changed hands between Britain and France – how many times? I forget. The roads were just as in India: narrow and overcrowded with pedestrians and cyclists. Apart from the mountainous centre, the island seems to be one vast sugar cane plantation. That's not quite fair; there are dozens of gorgeous beaches, lush hotels and casinos, but that is the point, it is very much a resort. Queen Victoria stands proudly with crown and sceptre outside Government House in Port Louis. Le Reduit, the Governor General's country house built in 1778, is a perfect gem of a two storey verandahed colonial delight; 300 gardeners are still employed. Also a delight are the gardens of Pamplemousse, where the Victoria Regina lilies spread their giant plates of floating leaves, strong enough, they say, to support a child.

27

France in Canada

The Moving Finger writes, and having writ,
Moves on: nor all they Piety nor Wit
Shall lure it back to cancel half a line,
Nor all thy Tears wash out a word of it.

The Rubaiyat of Omar Khayyam, Stanza 51

Two of my eight great grand-children live in Canada, so it was natural that we should make frequent expeditions, always driving ourselves in this Dominion so ideal for motoring. With two provisos: one that we avoid the winter which lasts an uncomfortable six months (though oddly enough, excellent wine is grown in Ontario Province, around Niagara); and two, that we impose ourselves for no more than two days on the family, ever mindful of the Chinese proverb already quoted.

I can't think why Toronto has acquired, in some quarters, a reputation for being 'boring'. Apart from its perfect position on Lake Ontario, its centre is compact, with all the hotels, restaurants, theatres and showplaces (like the 1,800ft high CN Tower) you could wish for but also one of the finest zoos, and unquestionably the finest Science Museum anywhere, with endless fascination from working demonstrations that will make your hair stand on end, literally!

Driving north, you are quickly into the Lake District, where fishermen hop about by seaplane, and into Algonquin National Park, a wilderness area. The Great Lakes extend to the west, and the St Lawrence river carries you away to the east, to Ottawa, Montreal and Quebec. However, enough of promotion. What I want to remind you of is Canada's duality; the reason that all announcements and advertisements must be expressed in French and English. Not that this carries much weight in Victoria, British Columbia, which is often described as 'more English than England'. Quite simply, French and English were always in rivalry over Canada. In 1497, John Cabot was exploring the 'new world' with a charter from King Henry VII; in 1534 Jacques Cartier sailed from Brittany with the same objective. It was all about a little animal, the beaver, so prized for its fur that it was hunted, with native Indian aid, almost to extinction.

On the Atlantic coast, fishing was of equal if not more importance; the harvesting of cod from the Grand Banks of Newfoundland being the prize for which English and French competed. During the eighteenth century, our Navies were more often at war than at peace, and a most interesting military relic is preserved as a tourist site at Louisbourg in Nova Scotia. As a half-Scot (my mother was a Mackay) I feel at home in the Province where more Gaelic is spoken than in Scotland. Cape Breton Island, which the French called Isle Royale, was strongly fortified at Louisbourg, and in the wars that followed it was besieged and changed hands twice. At the second capitulation, the British forces, comprising New Englanders supported by the Royal Navy, destroyed the town and Vauban's fortress. The garrison and nearly 8,000 civilians were shipped back to France.

Only within the last 20 years, has the fortress been restored and transformed into one of the finest working models of an eighteenth-century town and fort; not quite so large as, but on a par with, colonial Williamsburg in America. On the same principles, the aim is not only to replace the stones and fortifications, but the contemporary way of life, complete with people in traditional costumes.

The almost circular Cape Breton island, about the size of the Isle of Wight, is an appendage to the long narrow Province of Nova Scotia, and thereby hangs a tale. The narrow passage between island and mainland was a regular seaway, a short cut into the mouth of the St Lawrence. One foggy night, when a skipper was carefully conning his ship through the passage by means of his chart, he was startled to find his progress impeded by a very solid road bridge. Which only emphasises the importance of maps – that they should be up to date.

The modern village of Louisbourg is still a fishing harbour, with a great reputation for lobsters. Here you must park your car, for the only modern transport into Old Louisbourg is the visitor bus which deposits you at the drawbridge of Porte Dauphine. After being challenged by an officer and sentry in the uniforms of the Compagnie Franche de la Marine, you are free to wander the grid-pattern streets, the quays where ships were unloaded into the 'King's Storehouse', and the massive fortress with its ramparts and glacis. The King's Bastion with its casemates and demilunes faced inward, and being overlooked by higher ground, was of little use in resisting the bombardment of the 4,000 New England Volunteers when they took the fort in 1745 and proceeded to pound the town. It took only three weeks of shelling to bring about surrender.

The victory was a hollow one for the New Englanders, 1,000 of whom perished from famine and disease that winter. Three years later Louisbourg was restored to France by the Treaty of Aix la Chapelle. However, France and Britain were soon at war again, and in 1758 Louisbourg faced a more professional attack by 16,000 troops under Brigadier General James Wolfe – the victor in Quebec the following year. This time the British ordered the complete destruction of the fort, and thus it remained for 200 years.

Thanks to a vast store of French records and correspondence, now in the archives of Parks Canada, many buildings have been reconstructed on original foundations and in the finest detail. The main barracks, long two-storey buildings, contain the men's stark dormitories where they slept two to a wooden bunk, on straw changed once a year. In the centre are offices and a prison, a chapel and a priest's house, and officers' quarters – though most married officers lived in the town. At the far end of the block is the luxurious house of the Governor. The drawing room, dining room, bedroom, kitchen and council chamber are all furnished in authentic detail, down to the cooking implements, mainly originals researched from the *bricolage* shops of France. So much detail is known, including the very names of individual soldiers, that the uniformed 'animators' who show visitors round have been briefed to show the lazy, surly, untidy character of the men often conscripted from prisons, and condemned to a life of hardship and boredom with no relief but drinking. In the town we know who was the baker, the blacksmith, the armourer, the grocer, the laundry women, who was imprisoned for drunkenness. In the Chief Engineer's house you may find the maids cooking and eating a meal in his lavish kitchen and children weeding the herb garden. You may take an eighteenth-century lunch in the Auberge de l'Epée Royale: onion soup, boiled chicken, rice and carrots, bread pudding, bread and cheese, wine, brandy or rum. On Fridays, only fish. But the home-baked bread is a treat. This is history brought alive.

Go back a century earlier, in Ontario, and you will find history of a very different kind, on the shores of Georgian Bay at the eastern end of Lake Huron. The forested area of Muskoka is a playground of beaches, islands and yachting harbours, where floatplanes are parked as casually as a car. Here was founded the Jesuit Mission of Sainte Marie among the Hurons, which flourished between 1639 and 1749; then languished for three centuries, overgrown and forgotten.

Canada's keen sense of history has produced the Huronia Historical Park, which re-creates the life of fur traders, trappers and priests in the 'New France' of the seventeenth century. It is amazing that such a lonely outpost of European civilisation could be established, 800 miles from Quebec and 2,000 miles from the Atlantic, only 31 years after France's first precarious toehold at Quebec. But the close links between Church and State in feudal France made her colonisation almost as much a missionary as a military affair.

Before Samuel de Champlain, France's great soldier and administrator, had paddled up the Ottawa River and over 35 land portages to Georgian Bay, missionaries and fur traders had preceded him. In 1639, Jesuits then working among the Huron tribes, built Ste Marie as a permanent base. The Hurons were of a slightly more pacific disposition than the 'Five Nations' of the Iroquois, who live south of Lake Ontario, in what is now New York State. The Hurons were cultivators, where the Iroquois were hunters and nomads. The Huron birchbark canoes, laden with beaver pelts, would paddle down the Ottawa River to the annual Fair at Three Rivers or Montreal, but the Iroquois, armed by Dutch traders in Albany (New York) would ambush them and seize their goods. They took many a Huron scalp. The Mission was constantly under attack, and was defended by wooden palisades with bastions. The reconstructed buildings are mainly of wood, but partly in stone. The dormitory, refectory and chapel are flanked by a forge and carpenter's shop, both equipped and working. At first, vertical boards were used, but the cracks let in the piercing winds of winter, so a double skin of horizontal boards was added and filled with rubble for insulation. As many as 6,000 Indians would attend the Mission in the course of a year. The Jesuits lodged them in a longhouse built in Huron style, with saplings bent over to form a framework, covered in bark. There were shelves along the sides spread with furs to form beds, and cooking fires for several families ranged down the middle, smoke escaping through holes in the roof. All is faithfully reproduced, and a film based on the diary of the Mission's cobbler brings alive the daily life of the Mission.

Eventually the raiding parties of Iroquois overran Huronia, wiping out the entire Huron tribe of between 20,000 and 30,000, and burning six of the Jesuit priests. Sadly the surviving Jesuits put the torch to their home of ten years, and with a few faithful Huron converts, retreated to Quebec. A modern church dedicated to the six martyrs stands nearby.

Huronia did not disappear from history, however, for the Napoleonic Wars which brought America in on the side of France, turned the Great Lakes into an arena of naval battles. The Royal Navy having been defeated by the Americans on Lake Erie in 1813, there remained only one small British trading schooner, the *Nancy*, armed with three guns. Hunted by three heavily-armed American warships, she took refuge in the mouth of the Nottawasaga River, protected by a narrow wooded sandbank. Discovered here by the American Squadron, she was sunk by gunfire lobbed over the woods; but not before her resourceful Captain, Lieut Miller Worsley, RN had withdrawn his crew of 54 sailors and Indians. They then *rowed* 360 miles across Lake Huron to Michilimackinac, and there surprised and captured, from their rowboats, two American ships.

The burnt-out hulk of the *Nancy* lay gathering silt for 113 years, by which time an island had formed around her, on which now stands the Museum of the Upper Lakes. The *Nancy*'s hull was exhumed in 1928, and with models and mementoes, plus a sound and light reenactment of the engagement, is a memorial to a little-known exploit of the Royal Navy.

28

With Murphy, into Mexico

It must have been at my Prep School that a book prize for history happened to be W.H. Prescott's *Conquest of Mexico*, from which derived an early prejudice against Spain, because of the cruelty of the Conquistadors to the native subjects of Montezuma, coupled with admiration for the bravery and enterprise of Columbus in 'discovering' America. Ignoring for the moment that Columbus was not a Spaniard but a native of Genoa, this indicates all too clearly how the smallest mistakes and wrong impressions give rise to deeply-held but unfounded beliefs. It also seemed to a schoolboy unfair that Cortés had the advantage of cavalry, given that horses were strange beasts that the Aztecs had never seen. They were so puzzled by them that at first they believed man and horse to be one animal. Then there was the Aztec myth of the god Quetzalcoatl, the Plumed Serpent who would come from the east, which seemed to fit in with the pallid features of the Spaniards, so that they were not quite sure whether they were fighting men or magicians.

The effect of all these garbled impressions on a young mind was to instil a healthy scepticism for all history, and contributed the burning desire (which still remains) to visit all foreign countries and discover for myself what they and their inhabitants are really like.

Mexico is a good example of an early colonial country which has run full circle to independence, in only 300 years from Hernán Cortés' conquest of Tenochtitlán in 1521. Not exactly clean-cut independence, because there were a lot of complications. For one thing, Spanish Mexico extended well into what is now the USA. California, Utah, Arizona, Colorado, Nevada, and New Mexico all had to be ceded before Mexico could assume its present shape. And of course there had to be a guerilla struggle by native leaders, including Santa Anna who made himself President in 1833, and the greatest, Benito Juarez, who won the Civil War in 1861. By which time, Europe as well as America had its finger in the pie. France sent troops to support whoever was in power and could protect their trade. Emperor Franz Josef of Austria (so long-lived that he figures in two centuries of history), sent his younger brother Archduke Maximilian to be Governor of Mexico. Poor chap, he only lasted three years before being executed in 1867 by Juarez. Meanwhile the French had been exploring down the Mississippi to find new homes for their citizens expelled by the British from Canada, resulting in the French-speaking Louisiana, which had eventually to be bought by the USA. The 'Louisiana Purchase' was a good bargain for the hard faced Yankees, like that of Alaska. As for we British, we didn't meddle too much in that area, being satisfied with our Caribbean colonies, and the trade in sugar and slaves that brought so much wealth through the ports of Liverpool and Bristol. And so, Mexico entered the twentieth century still fighting – this time Francisco Madero was the revolutionary – and remains, for most Europeans, the romantic land of *mañana*, of burros, sombreros, cacti, and sleepy afternoons in sun-drenched plazas.

Pardon the eruption of half-digested history, but it is only by relating a few follies to each other that any sense can be made of the madness of current politics in Europe. If history teaches anything, it is that all attempts to force nations of very different peoples to cohabit are doomed to failure.

Think of Mexico and you think of pyramids; not indeed those pyramids of Egypt, but truncated ones, on whose flat tops horrifying sacrifices took place. Priests of the Maya or Toltecs, predecessors of the Aztecs, demanded the hearts of living victims to satisfy Huitzilopochtli, one of their strange gods which included Quetzalcoatl the Plumed Serpent.

Such gloomy thoughts were far from my mind when I hit Mexico City, for there was a festival which drew thousands of peasants into the great city, then 'only' of 10 million – for this was 30 years ago. Goodness knows how many it holds today, under an almost permanent blanket of smog and gridlocked traffic. There would be no room for the throngs of peasants in their brightly-coloured *sarapes*, carrying bundles of clothes, cooking pots and foodstuffs, as they camped out before the old Basilica of Guadalupe, which was then so threatened with collapse by earthquake tremors that it was very soon closed. The next time I saw Mexico City there was a brand-new Basilica, in a pleasingly modern style: Circular, with stained-glass all round. The dome is filled with slatted wood rising to a central point. Ingenious lighting consists of hexagonal tubes hanging from the ceiling, with onyx bases and slots in the sides to emit the light. To cope with the enormous crowds, an escalator trundles the pilgrims past the statue of the Virgin.

For balletophiles, Mexico is a happy hunting ground, for they have a rich tradition of folklore, kept very much alive by the National Ballet Folklorico in the Palace of Fine Arts. And in several other cities there were colourful shows. Perhaps the most dramatic was the 'Flying' of 'Los Voladores' which was performed after dark at Taxco. Not really a dance, but an enactment of a tradition attributed to the Totonacs of Papantla, who used to 'fly' their victims before sacrifice. The ceremony involves four men sitting on a platform on top of a 70ft-high pole, with ropes wound round and round their legs to such a length as to reach the ground. Having set the platform on top

132

gently revolving, the four men simultaneously hurl themselves off, head-first, and descend bearing torches, with the circular motion projecting their descent by centrifugal force outwards, so that they reach the ground in a wide circle. By a lucky shot, I managed to capture three out of the four in mid-descent, in black and white. The descent takes several minutes, as the ropes slowly unwind, like a slowed-up bungee jump. A fifth man remains playing the flute on top of the pole.

By another lucky chance in Mexico City, a German TV company was filming a professional dance troupe in the Plaza of Three Cultures, so called because in the same square are found an Aztec temple, a Spanish colonial church, and blocks of very modern flats. In a Moorish dance from Patzcuaro, which is supposed to bring good luck to the local fishermen, a group of nine men were dressed in black velvet tunics and trousers, embroidered with silver fishes. On their heads they wore formalised turbans surmounted by crescents and a star. A *mariachi* band provided a haunting and repetitive little tune.

The *Llorona*, or 'Whipping' dance, comes from Oaxaca province, and symbolises a woman who has lost her child at sea, and found only its dress. Hence they wear a child's white lace dress as headdress. Their costumes are brightly embroidered with flowers on a black background, and they carry baskets of artificial flowers, while their men partners wear pink jackets and carry tall silver crosses. Outside the church, they made a striking tribute to Christianity. Just why the Moors should have been represented in the Patzcuaro dance is not clear; and another odd feature of their costume is that the men's faces are all encased in a dark-blue diaphanous veil. Homage to two religions? But the Moors, or Muslims, were never involved, so far as I know, with Mexico.

The tourist trail in Mexico is rightly linked to its history, for that is one of the world's oldest and most interesting. Close to Mexico City lies the religious city of Teotihuacan, where the Street of the Dead runs between the Pyramids of the Sun and the Moon. The former has roughly the same base area as the great Pyramid of Khufu at Giza, but it is so much lower that the flat top had room for the sacrificial buildings of the priests, whose skill with their obsidian knives was such that they could extract a victim's heart and offer it to the gods while it was still beating. All these buildings were of course cleared away by Cortés. In their endeavour to obtain maximum height, the builders made the steps so narrow that it is a physical effort to climb up, and an even greater risk going down.

The same applies to all the pyramids of Central America, and at Uxmal near Merida in Yucatan, the Pyramid of the Magician is even taller and steeper. While climbing it, there was a French girl and her mother, also ascending with some difficulty. Arriving at a level terrace near the top, the girl was afflicted with a complete freeze of vertigo, and was unable to look anywhere but at the wall. With another man to help, we had quite a job getting her down. It was essential she remained facing the stone; she could not look out, even at the sky, much less the ground. So we had to steady her feet on the steps, putting each foot in turn on a lower step, until eventually we reached terra firma safely. Meanwhile her mother had left her daughter to our care, and nimbly descended on her own.

In the Yucatan area, the pyramids, temples and cenotes (or holy lakes) into which gold offerings were cast, are Mayan, rather than Aztec, and older. It is remarkable how well preserved are the stone carvings, many showing Tlaloc the rain god, or Quetzalcoatl. There are ball courts, with a stone ring through which a rubber ball had to be passed; whether the victors were rewarded or sacrificed is a matter of dispute by the expert historians.

At Guanajuato, a handsome little town in a valley, entered via an underground street, it was possible to visit a silver mine. Marfil had once been the richest in Mexico, with 30,000 workers. In 1905 a week's excessive rainfall caused the river to flood, wrecking the town and mine, and drowning 2,000 people. Marfil became a ghost town and the mine was never rebuilt; but at the new mine I put on belt and helmet for lamp, and descended 1,400ft in an open cage to walk along roads where men pushed wagons of ore, past a chapel, to a working face. Although dusty, it had the merit of being white and clean-looking compared to a coal mine. At the surface mill where crushers grind up the ore, it is curious to find that silver is produced from a lake of black sludge which ends up like small lumps of coal. Further processing is obviously then carried out which I did not have time to follow up. Rather similar to the processing of tin in Malaya.

The wealth of Guanajuato shows up in elegant houses and fine churches such as the Churrigesque La Compania, built in 1765, and a striking white University dating from 1732. Above all, I loved the Juarez Theatre, a square building on a terrace decorated with metalwork and palm trees. It had a plump Victorian solidity appropriate to its date: 1850.

Guadalajara is another big city much favoured by American visitors and residents. One of its attractions is the Charreada, Mexico's version of the Calgary Stampede, a festival of the horse, with lassoing, bareback bull-riding, roping of steers, and trick riding. Best of all for a balletophile is the University which has a Department of Fine Arts which maintains the 'Grupo Folklorico de la Universidad de Guadalajara' and to crown my luck, the students were holding a rehearsal in a sunny patio, so had time to repeat movements ad lib for my cameras. These beautiful young people in colourful costumes yielded superb results in traditional dances, such as the Jarabe Tapatio of Jalisco Province, the girls in skirts that balloon when they swirl, and the men in tight black trousers and straw hats.

In the Corridos de Seis Minas (Ballet of Six Miners) the dancers dress dates from the 'naughty nineties', the girls in long skirts and the men in jackets and tight trousers, with wide-brimmed straw hats rising to a point. This dance includes a chain movement. From Oaxaca in the south comes the Dance of the Plumes, a high leaping dance of the Zapotec Indians, danced by a soloist

Kyonghoeru Pavilion, part of Kyongbok Palace, Seoul

The Royal Band, court musicians in National costume, Changdok Palace, Seoul

National costume at the Korean Folk Festival

Changdok Palace. The intricate eaves are built without nails

Changdok Palace, entrance gate

Procession with decorations for Besakhi
Temple

Sita dances in centre of chorus of chanting
men in Ketchak dance

Barong and Hanuman entertain the village children

Water must be carried up 300 steps at
Gunung Kawi

Carrying home the paddy for threshing

ura Kehen. Eleven tiers make it a very holy
mple

Mask of Chalonarang

Sanur beach. The finest white beach in Bali

Prahus (outrigger canoes)

The Ketchak dance, Hanuman the monkey God saves Sita

A white Bull carries a Brahim priest to his cremation

Temple of Heaven

Imperial Dragon

Gate of Heavenly purity in the forbidden city, Peking

Stone boat built for the Empress Tzu Shi at the summer Palace
Peking

The Great Wall writhes like a snake. Note steepness of steps at
bottom right hand corner

Sampan sailing on the Li river

Chungking passenger harbour on the Yangtse

Clouds hang in the Gorges on the Yangtse river

er steamer on the Yangtse of 2300 tons, she carries
passengers

Poling a Sampan on the Li river

MS Lycianda in the Yasawa Isles

Leonard the captain dancing with a passenger

Yasawa Islanders make fine handicrafts of baskets and shells

Going ashore at Nanuya Lailai

Fijian Police Band serenading a cruise liner at Suva

Fijian Meke, Yanuca island

South Pacific hairstyle. Hibiscus and Frangipani,
Yasawa isles

Daughter follows mum to work

Who she? nothing to do with elephants. She's here because she's irresistibly Thai

Elephant bath

War elephants at the Surin round-up

The King leads war elephants at the Surin round-up

Mother elephants reassure their babies only a few weeks old, scared by a barking dog

Saint Panteleimon, Russian Monastery

iests in Katholikon, Saint Panteleimon

Father Avil from Soviet Union, and two visiting Russians. On right: Dimitri Rechkalo from Sydney was my companion and translator

The Katholikon

ie Bakery at Karyes, delivery by donkey

The merry Monk

On the Palace ridge, Tananarive

The upside down tree A Baobab
(Adamsonia Madagascariensis)

Wooden memorial of Antanosy tribe,
Fort Dauphin

Tananarive, Malagasy

A Mauritius beach

Victoria Regina lilies, Pamplemousse gardens, Mauritius

csahuaman. Massive stones of Inca fortress above Cuzco, Peru

Machu Picchu 'Lost city' of the Incas, Peru

uassu Falls from Argentine side

Iguassu Falls from Brazil side

anish cathedral and Governor's Palace, Quito, Ecuador

Copacabana beach, Rio de Janeiro, Brazil

Guard inspection in the Fortress, Louisbourg,
Nova Scotia

King's Bastion, Louisbourg

Porte Dauphine rebuilt as in 1744

The Council chamber

St James in the Lines, Garrison church, built 1836.
Penetanguishene. Georgian Bay, Lake Huron

Algonquin Wigwam of bark, and church for Indian
converts. Sainte Marie among the Hurons, Jesuit
mission

odel of HMS Nancy, British Warship sunk by the Americans
1814 in Lake Huron. Her burnt hulk formed an island
ich is now a museum

First canal in Canada. Built by Jesuit fathers in 1639, behind is
the church, Sainte Marie

Three generations Pilgrim time, Basilica of Guadaloupe, Mexico City

Carnival time, Merida

Killing time, Mexico City

Country time, two on a Burro Taxco

Mayan girl in a Huipil. Her children in Japanese costume for carnival Xocchel near Merida

Mexican hat! Folklore group of Guadalahara University

Jarabe Tapatio. Dance of Jalisco province by folklore group of Guadalahara University

Moors and Christians represented by costume decorations. Folk dance of Patzcuaro in Mexico City

Tlaloc the rain God

A Chichimec Indian on pilgrimage at San Juan de los Lagos

Coatlicue, Goddess of death and fertility

with scarlet jacket and gaudy circular headdress of red and yellow, fringed with green feathers. There is also a charming love dance between a couple dressed in white, originating in Vera Cruz on the Caribbean coast, where Cortés landed. All these are authentic and traditional folk dances, most of which I saw performed again in the Palace of Fine Arts in Mexico City.

Ballet apart, the two things not to be missed in Mexico City are Chapultepec Castle, the gracious home of Maximilian and his wife Carlotta, with two walls covered by murals depicting hundreds of historical characters, including the surrender of the Emperor and various revolutionary leaders, and the Museum of Anthropology, itself a superb modern building with a circular metal roof from which descends a curtain of water. Inside, the many displays of ancient artifacts, models and maps give an excellent idea of Mexico's very ancient history, races and religions.

Not forgetting Mexico's long Pacific coast, I drove down to Acapulco which was then somewhat like the French Riviera of the 1920s, just becoming fashionable. Now, alas, it is a desert of high-rise condominiums and hotels, the hang-out of the American 'bucket and spade' holidaymaker, with not much to see but parasailing and the high divers at Quebrada. Further north, into the long peninsula Baja California, which is physically part of California but belongs to Mexico, tourism spreads with the novelty of Ixtapa and Mazatlan, and the old grey whales swim down from the Arctic to calve in the shallow waters inside the Gulf of California.

Sometimes Murphy's Law prevails, and I feel my middle name must be Murphy. At other times, a Guardian Angel seems to hover over my wayward steps. One place where Murphy invariably inhabits is India, where an uncertain outcome to all human endeavour is likely to arise from any activity, whether from weather, communications, both human and mechanical, misunderstanding of language, incompetence or the confusion of wish for reality.

The Guardian Angel unexpectedly appeared in Mexico. But there was no reason to expect any divine or other assistance when I crashed my hire car on a lonely country road near Guanajuato. The road ran straight and level across a dull dry landscape of sparse bushes, cactus and sisal, from which Tequila is brewed. There were two cars ahead of me, close together and driving extremely slowly. The road ahead was clear, an inviting chance to pass a slowcoach, so I pulled out, with a toot on my horn. At that precise moment, the rearward of the pair ahead decided to do the same, forcing me to veer way over to the left side. Unfortunately this main road consisted of a narrow blacktop with shoulders of soft gravel. The sudden swerve into soft gravel caused me to skid, and correcting the skid back onto the tarmac with a shade too much rudder after having passed the two cars, induced a skid on the near side. The road was a ridge-road, in effect running on an embankment, so by now proceeding backwards, I slid off into a ditch about 6ft deep. The other two drivers must have seen my strange disappearance from view but took no

135

notice. On getting out to survey the situation, I found the ditch was steep, and full of large boulders. There was no question of getting out without assistance.

The situation seemed, as the Viennese say, 'desperate but not serious'. Several cars ignored my appeals for help. The only people who stopped were two boys on a motor bike and four peasant lads on two horses (two lads on each horse). We jacked up the car and moved a large boulder from underneath, disclosing that one front wheel had broken off. The situation was now both desperate and serious.

Many more cars ignored my signals to stop, until eventually my Guardian Angel appeared, in the form of English-speaking Doctor Pedro Valencia. He took me back to his home in Yuriria, where he said there were only five doctors for 10,000 people, or 40,00 if you include the surrounding country-side. He was a pediatrician and had four children. Cost of living was not onerous, he said. Servants cost only 100 pesos a month (about £3.50) and he had two of them. Dr Valencia called up a breakdown truck, which arrived in the care of Liborio Almanza, and we went to inspect the wreck. Liborio refused to touch it without permission from the Transito Police, so we drove into the nearest town and spent 40 minutes on what the Doctor said would take five; waiting for a policeman to make out a written chit (raising an infraction) and collecting 10 pesos *propina*. We hurried back to my car, but it was already sunset, and towing is not allowed after dark. This did not seem to worry Liborio however. The four Campesinos who had remained on guard all this time, were despatched with a *pourboire* of 50 pesos between them, and set off happily on their two bareback horses. The ever-to-be-blessed Dr Valencia then drove me 22 miles to a comfortable motel, having accomplished an act of benevolence that went far beyond the call of duty, and for which he refused payment except for the considerable cost of telephone calls. Next day, Avis arrived with a replacement car and I was on my way. It was an experience which really restored my faith in the human condition.

However, Murphy had not finished with me. On a tight schedule which involved leaving Cancun on the Atlantic coast, to fly right across Mexico to investigate new resorts just opening up at Ixtapa and Mazatlan on the Pacific, the flight left at 7 a.m. with a change of planes at Merida, the main town of the Yucatan district. Here there turned out to be a wait for the best part of a day, ample time to revisit Uxmal, the Mayan pyramid site where I'd had the adventure with the giddy French girl. There was plenty more to see there.

After a hassle with a group of taxi drivers, a deal was struck with a beat-up old Ford, and the first thing the driver did was to go to a filling station and buy several cans of oil, and fill up the radiator with gallons of water. Ominous signs, as I should have guessed. After an hour on the road, it was obvious that we were heading for Chichen Itza, not Uxmal. Hardly had we turned round, on a bare cactus-strewn plain with not a shade tree in sight, and the temperature in the nineties, when there was a bang and the engine blew up in a cloud of smoke and steam and smell of burning metal. Pouring water in was useless, as it went straight through.

Situation desperate but not serious? Well, not really serious, for my Guardian Angel turned up in a truck, and ferried me back to Merida (without charge). In good time to catch my plane.

Some you win; some you lose. Sometimes we have to accept the smooth with the rough. Thanks, Murphy.

29

South American Roundabout

Yes, weekly from Southampton,
Great Steamers, white and gold,
Go rolling down to Rio,
(Roll down, Roll down to Rio).

Kipling

When things go wrong on a foreign trip, there's always an explanation: sheer carelessness, sheer ignorance, sheer accident, sheer bloody-mindedness, sheer bad luck. Take your pick. The secret is, however, to accept all the muck thrown at you, and come out smelling of roses.

On a three-week tour of South America, taking in five countries, it's reasonable to expect some downsides: long flights, early starts, changed schedules, bad weather, incompetent guides, reserved rooms that aren't, excessive heat and air-conditioning that doesn't work. But, *per contra*, there are new customs, new languages, some superb food, fantastic sights, breathtaking scenery, many reminders of history, and, for me, a voyage on the highest lake in the world.

An all-night flight, and it's a rather abrupt elevation to 9,250ft on landing at Quito in Ecuador. A good modern hotel, but photography comes before rest, so I hasten to explore this rather fine capital of a former Spanish colony. The Governor's Palace, Cathedral, and Archbishop's Palace, strive to outdo each other in magnificence. The gold the Spaniards sought was turned into some very beautiful examples of colonial architecture: cloisters, monasteries, dazzling gilt altars; La Compahnia Church is covered in gold leaf from walls to ceiling. In La Conception, with a service in progress, there is pleasant singing coming from the nuns' enclosure high up at the back.

Excursion to the Equator where we stand with a foot in each hemisphere. A pleasantly green and fertile country, where potatoes are planted in the traditional way, one by one, with a hand-held and foot-operated plough. A three-man or woman job; one operating the plough, a second dropping a handful of fertiliser and a third the spud in the hole. In the markets the women all wear ponchos and felt hats, with babies strapped on their backs. Petrol, I note, is 11p a gallon.

Lima in Peru finds us at sea level, and in a city where poverty is all-enveloping. Enormous delays at airport due to mad system of four separate customs checks, and exit through a single narrow doorway where everyone lines up with all their baggage. Streets filthy, made worse by a dustmen's strike. Dust covers even the leaves of trees. A bad beginning, for the Inca's Revenge has already struck, and I am on Streptotriad and lemon tea.

Next day, breakfastless, we are on the coach tour to Pachacamac, a pre-Inca ruin on the coast, a desolate desert where it never rains. The guide's strident voice, muffled by the microphone and unintelligible, never lets up for a second; four hours of hell. A huge city, still largely unexcavated, surrounds the Temple of the Sun, a mound which yielded 400 loads of gold for the ransom of the Inca Atahuallpa, who was so shamefully cheated and executed by Pizarro.

Lima yielded some fine colonial buildings, notably the Archbishop's Palace and Town Hall which have fretted wooden balconies. The Ethnological Museum is noted for its pre-Inca pottery, jewellery and gold objects, as well as mummies and skulls which show evidence of trepanning. Dinner is the first food I have eaten for 32 hours.

The flight to Cuzco takes us into the Andes, whose 20,000ft peaks rival the Himalayas. Cuzco, the capital of the last Inca, Atahuallpa, is a city of red-tiled roofs between steeply terraced hill sides. It is full of evidence of the skill of Inca stonemasons whose feats rival those of the ancient Egyptians. There are the same huge stones, fitted together with mathematical precision, despite irregular shapes, so that a knife cannot be passed between them. A supreme example is the street of Hatun Rumiyoc, where one stone has 12 corners, each perfectly fitted to its neighbour. On a larger scale, the fortress of Sacsay-huaman, which as the guide explains, is pronounced roughly as 'Sexywoman', is built of blocks 10ft or more high, piled upon each other, and weighing up to 50 tons.

Touring around Cuzco showed how industriously the Incas had terraced their steep mountain country, almost up to the peaks, though the highest levels are no longer cultivated. There are fortified villages, storehouses for grain, and public baths, showing a high level of sophistication. In fact, the Incas had a sort of social service system involving the storing of adequate reserves of essential foodstuffs, tools and clothing. Records were kept by a unique system of knotted cords called *quipus*, by which the exact number of goods in every storehouse was known. And of course the Incas were noted for their 'postal' system of runners always kept in readiness, who could relay messages from end to end of the kingdom within a few days. It is interesting to remember that the Mongols had a similar system, whereby Genghis Khan and his grandson Tamerlane could control the rapid movements of their armies across the plains and mountains, from China, through Mongolia, to

Persia and Turkey. It is the juxtaposition of such similarities that makes travel, with a historically-oriented eye, so fascinating. Compared to our modern scientific inventions, subject to breakdown by a power failure, or damage by nature, fire or flood, the old ways were probably more reliable!

The high-point of our journey was now upon us: the 'lost city' of Machu Picchu which Pizarro never discovered. So steep are the surrounding mountains, that the city is invisible from the valleys. The narrow-gauge train is a bonus for railway nuts. A big orange diesel loco, with 12 driving wheels, independently sprung, starts off with four zig-zags to gain height, then climbs with many tight curves, up to 12,000ft before dropping to 6,000ft at the base station, under 3,000ft cliffs on each side. Thence minibuses carry the tourists up to a narrow saddle straddled by the ruined city at about 7,350ft, so well-known from countless photographs. Though roofless, most of the houses, the Inca's Palace, the Sun temple are still intact. Terraces were cultivated, with different soils imported to suit the various crops. Hiram Bingham rediscovered the city in 1911.

Most visitors are on a day trip, but we were lucky to have reservations at the tiny hotel, so we woke to the majestic solitude of a circle of mountain tops enveloped in cloud and mist, which soon cleared, to give us an unimpeded run of the hundreds of royal, priestly and domestic buildings that must have housed thousands of people.

The next leg of our South American odyssey is a long one: 3,380kms by rail to Juliaca and Lake Titicaca, which forms the boundary between Peru and Bolivia. For the next few days we are going to be living at about 14,000ft, almost the height of Mont Blanc. Some people are affected by such heights, but I suffered no shortage of breath; on the contrary I found it stimulating, and spent much of the long train journey on the open platform at the end of the coach, watching the scattered llamas and alpacas grazing on the tussock grass on desolate treeless slopes of the *altiplano*.

At Puno the glassy expanse of Lake Titicaca, a deep blue, lay under a brilliant sky, the highest navigable lake in the world, and almost at the dead centre of the continent. Here things started to go wrong. Mismanagement by local agents and hotels left unhonoured bookings, and a search for beds which left some of us (not me) in hotels with no water, no lavatory and no breakfast! With the vast expanse of the lake at hand, it seemed strange that water was only turned on for a few hours morning and night.

We crossed the lake by hydrofoil, stopping at Sun Island and passing a station of the Bolivian Navy, for the lake has long been navigated by steamers, and it is after all an international frontier. Our main interest was in the reed boats or canoes which were the model for Thor Heyerdahl's Pacific crossing. Small examples are still made and used by fishermen on the lake.

It was now only a fairly short distance by bus to La Paz, capital of Bolivia, which lies at the bottom of a steep crater. The road was very bad and often narrow. At one bottleneck we were confronted by a lorry which refused to give way or back up. Our driver got out to argue with the lorry driver, but I thought of another way. I also got out and photographed the driver, telling him I was taking his portrait to the police. It worked immediately.

La Paz was a disaster, indeed a washout. We were due for a two-night stay, and there were luxurious hotels such as the La Paz where I got one of six singles available. But all the doubles had to get back on the bus and search elsewhere. One of our ladies was ill with pneumonia, and a gentleman was beside himself with fury, wishing to sue everyone in sight. The hotel manager claimed that his rooms had been taken over by the government – an obvious lie; and next morning I made him confess that the mix-up was entirely the hotel's fault. Anyway, airline flight schedules had been changed, so that we could not stay the second night, but departed for Buenos Aires first thing next morning. *Adios*, La Paz, and no *hasta la vista*.

The airport at La Paz is at 13,695ft elevation, and we were there at 7.45 a.m. for a flight in a Lloyd Aero Boliviano Boeing 727, with a change of plane on the apron at Cochabamba, for Buenos Aires. It was like a return to civilisation; everything from Rachel the guide who met us, speaking perfect English, to the comfort of the Plaza Hotel. At 5 p.m. we had afternoon tea in the tearoom, complete with pianist; an enormous spread of sandwiches, fresh and toasted, scones, butter, jam, petits fours, and assorted cakes. A 1920s atmosphere to perfection. The biggest surprise was the 1920s price: because of galloping inflation the whole lot was 50p! And similarly with a fabulous dinner of fish, sirloin steak, spinach, avocado salad, pears and cream, all for under £2.

An extra day in Buenos Aires did nobody any harm, being devoted to sightseeing in the handsome city, shopping and feasting. We took the opportunity of giving a postponed birthday party to the lady who had been so ill on the real date three days before.

Though the Avenida Ninth July is wider than the Champs Élysées, there were monumental traffic jams, with free-for-alls at the junctions. Besides handsome government buildings, there are parks with lakes and pedalos, acacias, blue jacarandas and scarlet-flowered ceibo trees. The statue of Rodin's Thinker is one of his three originals; all the others scattered around the world are copies. A trip into the country showed us the pampass where the cowboys flourish on a diet of steaks and grilled testicles – according to tradition. A coach trip to the riverside suburbs of Olivos and San Isidro passed lovely houses and gardens, and a launch took us up the Tigre River, a tributary of the mighty Parana. Though Buenos Aires is 200 miles from the sea, the estuary of the River Plate on which it stands is so wide that Uruguay on the other side is quite invisible.

One more country remained, and that the biggest and hottest: Brazil. We were still in the Argentine when we landed at Iguacu in a temperature of 94°F for lunch at Las Cataratas Hotel before viewing the Falls which are the only reason for stopping. Reason enough, for they are one of the mightiest in

141

the world. Not for height, but for lateral size and extent, covering miles of a sheer escarpment in the jungle. Well-planned walkways enable one to approach to the very lip among the spray at several points. The Falls extend for miles up and down stream of the Parana, and plans for a dam, only just starting when we were there, have probably changed the scene by now. Motor boats ferried us across to the Brazilian side and a night stop in a hotel where the air-conditioning could not bring bedrooms below 88°F and the bar to 80°F. But there were more excellent views and walkways to the Falls. It was an uncomfortable night lying naked on my bed – just like India. The bath was so small that when I lay down in it, it overflowed.

On the flight to Rio with Varig the first hop was to São Paulo, twice the size of Rio, and we flew into such bad turbulence, with thunderstorms all around us, that we put down at Curitiba and waited an hour and a half for a lull. From São Paulo it was only a 50-minute shuttle flight to Rio, in a Viscount, that lovely old plane with big windows and plenty of room, only equalled by a Dakota. Landing at the domestic airport by the harbour, we were soon in our hotel on Copacabana Beach with its double promenade shaded by palms. There was the usual trouble over rooms; one lady being shown into a room with a man in bed. We soon found we were in Mañana country; it took from 9 to 11 p.m. to get one course, pineapple and coffee, from the dusky waitresses in creole dress. A trio beguiled us with sambas.

The usual sights included Sugar Loaf Mountain by cable car, and Corcovado with the statue of Christ, and a ferry boat to Paqueta Island, a beach resort with nice bungalows, but the water was polluted by oil from the many tankers. On Copacabana beach some of our ladies sunbathed, but one lost her handbag to boys who sneaked up, pretending to be digging sandpits while she dozed.

For a final flavour of South America there was a nightclub where four mulatto samba dancers did tricks with tambourines, and other sketches included slaves and voodoo. Many of the mulatto girls were very tall and handsome, in festival-type dress, and they indulged in much bottom-wiggling with men in the audience. When my turn came, my only protection was a cherry stick from my cocktail glass, but I found that when inserted in an appropriate place, it secured privacy.

Reel 6

The Drop of the Curtain

30

A Retrospective of India

The European official in India seldom, if ever,
sees anything in its real light, so dense is the veil
which the fearfulness, the duplicity, the prejudice, and
the superstitions of the natives hang before his eyes.

Sir Richard Burton

Nature fashioned Pakistan, India and Bangladesh as one country, or sub-continent if you prefer; but bits of it have often been ruled by assorted Satraps, of which the Satrapy of the East India Company and its successor the Satrapy of Queen Victoria were the most successful – though at no time was more than three fifths of the country under her direct rule. 562 princely states formed no part of the demand for 'liberation'.

 Over 92 years I have witnessed fundamental changes, even to the extreme of Partition; but in the time scale of history these are no more than par for the course. Since the time of Ashoka and Buddha, countless invasions have scattered the reins of power among tribes from Central Asia, Mongolia, Afghanistan, Persia, and the European tribes of Portugal, France and Great Britain. Religions and languages have permutated, divided and sub-divided into a mosaic of ever-changing civilisations. The intrusion of European tribes has merely stirred the melting pot, leaving its constituent parts the same. The Karma of the Hindu, always sure of rebirth, the cold logic of the Buddhist Wheel of Life, the perpetual Will of Allah, set in book form, are but lightly brushed with the saving grace of Christian belief in redemption and Heaven.

From all the mists of memory, the figures that stand out most clearly are the people of India; complex, illogical, corrupt, infuriating; but indestructible and unforgettable.

I see them all, from Maharajah to beggar, accepting their status according to caste or *dastur* (custom). For two generations they have been our brothers-in-arms. I remember the low caste Telegu villagers who lived in thatched huts just across the road from our RAF thatched huts; the red-coated railway porters who bore the heaviest loads on their heads for a fee of an anna or two; the

145

Malayalis in spotless white whose rope-making I watched under the palms of Malabar; the barefooted farmers who ploughed, reaped and threshed by hand, suffering famine in 1943 and narrowly averted it in the 1960s; the housewives who laboriously hauled water from the wells and carried it home on their heads; the University graduate met on a flight to Ahmedabad who engaged in philosophical discussion on all religions, the Christian bearer who served me so faithfully from 0630 *Chhota hazri* to 10 p.m. dinner; the Hindu priests who introduced me to the inner sanctum of the rat temple at Deshnoke, filled with huge bowls of grain, overrun by thousands of rats who are worshipped.

I respect Islam though reject its excesses, for nowhere in the Koran is *purdah* ordained for women. I respect the Sikhs whose beard and turban identify their hospitable faith which feeds travellers and rejects caste; the Buddhist monks whose doctrine of non-violence carries on that of Gandhi; the Christian nuns whose blue-bordered white saris betoken the charity of Mother Teresa, whom I met twice. I saw the destitutes, the 'poorest of the poor' as she called them, in her Home for the Dying at Kali Ghat, from which many of them actually recover. I accept the millions of Hindus who, irrespective of caste, seek their destiny by astrology, the most negative and retrospective of faiths. And then there are the Adivasi or tribal people, outside all caste or creed, whose lives are governed by propitiation of spirits. Taking no sides, I tried to understand them all.

Bombed by Pakistan

Other people's war souvenirs are usually a turnoff – unless you happen to have served in the same outfit. That is why I have not attempted any sequential record of my inglorious service abroad, while my wife remained at work as a Civil Servant in London, through all the successive blitzes, including V-Is and V-IIs. I never saw a shot fired in anger, or heard a bomb ... UNTIL ...

To be in a friendly country in peacetime, and to be bombed by that country's Air Force, with whose pilots you had previously flown – that's another matter.

At the end of another two months' tour of India in 1971 I was minding my own business in Jodhpur, in fact asleep in the Judges' Lodgings of the Circuit House, when I heard a sound not heard since the last war: the 'crump' of two bombs. Going out on to the balcony, there was a fusillade of ack-ack, with red tracer bullets crossing the sky like fireworks. My next door neighbour joined me on the balcony, with a portable radio, on which we heard the voice of Mrs Gandhi declaring that, following Pakistan's unprovoked attack, we were now at war. It reminded me of Chamberlain in 1939. If you are being bombed at night by an unseen opponent, there is not much you can do about it except go back to bed, which I did; remembering how in the very first days of 1940's Blitz on London, we once or twice went to the Andersen shelter, but soon gave it up as a waste of good sleep time.

At about 3.30 a.m. we were woken by a further salvo of bombs, and from the balcony were in time to see two planes junking and weaving just above the rooftops. They had been smart enough to approach from the east, so the bombs were dropped on their way home to Pakistan. A full moon made it almost as bright as day, and across the city on the airfield there was a big conflagration where a petrol dump had been hit, causing some damage and casualties. The glare from the fire lit up the Maharajah's great new sandstone palace, now a luxury hotel, and turned the ancient fort on a cliff overlooking the city to a vision of pink splendour.

My neighbour was a minor Rajah of the State of Sirohi, who by coincidence had that very day lost his title and privileges, withdrawn by Mrs Gandhi. His advice was to get out of India as quickly as possible; but seeing that all Indian Airlines internal flights had been cancelled, this was easier said than done. However, a taxi was procured, at the rather steep rate of one rupee a mile, to drive the 116 miles to Marwar Junction, to catch the Delhi Mail to Ahmedabad. There a change to the Saurashtra Express brought me in air-conditioned comfort, with lunch and dinner on the train (soup, chicken curry and rice) to a blacked-out Bombay by 9 a.m. The city was chaotic, but having secured an Air India reservation for 1 a.m. the next morning, I had a day to spare; well employed in a cinema for one of the best Bond films: *On Her Majesty's Secret Service*, with hilarious scenes in Switzerland; a stock-car race on a skating rink, and Bond and Blofeld chasing each other down the Cresta Run.

India's Maharajahs were having a struggle with Mrs Gandhi's government at this time, resisting her intention to deprive them of their rights which were enshrined in the historical treaties they or their forbears had made with the East India Company and the British government, and were preserved to a limited extent in 1947. Some accepted the changes with a good grace, and became politicians, finding easy acceptance in democratic voting because of their popularity with their former subjects. For example, Dr Karen Singh, the Maharajah of Kashmir, whom I met as Minister of Tourism served the government without drawing his salary. The Maharana of Mewar, on the other hand, whose Lake Palace Hotel at Udaipur is without doubt the most romantic and beautiful in India, was the leader of a group of rulers who resisted. He explained their policy to me with a booklet setting out the case for inviolate treaties. There was supposed to be a curse on Mewar, that no Maharana could father a child while ruling, and this had happened for the eighth time when I met Bhagwat Singh who was himself an adopted son. But he already had three children before he came to the *gadi* (throne), so his son could inherit. I also interviewed the Maharajah of Mysore. He was so wealthy that he had no cause to worry on that score, and seemed more interested in Hindu philosophy. At Bikaner I stayed in the Maharajah's Palace Hotel, and found him a keen and very expert photographer. His State had always been a model of good rule and modernity.

I spent a few days in the palace of the Maharajah of Bhavnagar, to whose father my brother had briefly served as Private Secretary before the war. Bhavnagar lies on the coast of Gujarat, and its principal wealth is salt. It was to Gujarat that Gandhi led his 'Salt March' to produce home-distilled salt in protest at the salt taxes. The modern young Maharajah has commercial interests in the film industry – 'Bollywood' in Mumbai, as Bombay is now called. Bhavnagar was one of the richest States for its size, and had its own state railway with an English General Manager. It also drew considerable customs duties from 400 miles of other railways which ran through the state.

Bhavnagar was one of the last four States to practise the sport of hunting black buck with cheetahs in the 1930s. The previous Maharajah kept a collection of 15 cheetahs, trained by a Muslim, and when they were taken out into the desert by car or cart, and one was released in sight of a black buck, the chase was swift and deadly, for none could outrun them. There was no cruelty because death was immediate, and if the cheetah missed, it was left free. The young Maharajah took me on a duck shoot, but all he got was one bird slightly wounded in the wing, which he took back to be cared for in his aviary.

My parents would have been as proud to receive an invitation from a Maharajah as from Lady Willingdon at Government House, but now the romance of medieval princely pomp is almost forgotten. The White Man's Burden is lifted, and I rejoice to see India free to govern herself.

Manna from Heaven

My idyllic love affair with Malabar in 1942 was soon to be curtailed. A signal from 225 Group demanded my return to Bangalore for immediate posting to Cuttack, a newly-opened RAF Station on the Bay of Bengal, about 200 miles south of Calcutta. Three officers were urgently required for Operations Room duties, and two others were being hastily summoned from other out-stations.

With my tin trunk, suitcase, and cumbrous bedding-roll containing camp bed and bedding, blankets, pillows, towels, portable washstand and chair, the expedition set off by rail via Madras. Here there was time for a leisurely lunch and a bathe at the club before attaining the main line, where the Madras-Calcutta Mail departs at night. The 48-hour journey to Cuttack was made entertaining by sharing a first-class compartment with a young Anglo-Burman Sub-Lieutenant in the Royal Indian Navy, whose Irish grandfather made him feel, as he expressed it, 101 per cent British. Three or four times in the day, the train stopped at station refreshment rooms for meals. Once by lamplight and under an old-fashioned punkah pulled by a coolie, we enjoyed a six course dinner. Not surprisingly, the overall journey speed for this 'Express' train was 20mph.

RAF Station Cuttack, which had two squadrons of Hudsons, was on a desolate plain of red laterite, 14 miles from the town by rutted earth roads and river beds which had just been flooded by the monsoon. My arrival, together with two other Intelligence Officers, Morgan and Cassidy, caused considerable surprise, for we were neither required nor requested. They had a full complement, and in any case had no Operations Room. While signals flew between their 221 Group Headquarters in Calcutta, and my 225 Group in Bangalore, to sort out the gremlins, we unwanted bodies contemplated the barren, treeless landscape where slit trenches were being dug by coolies, or cadged lifts on the rations truck into Cuttack town, a dismal spot, noted only for its craftwork of flashy silver jewellery.

Meanwhile we enjoyed the hospitality of the Officers' Mess, and their Field Service Rations; basically bully beef, biscuits and jam, supplemented by mysterious tinned objects resembling a sausage in shape, designated 'links', which formed our daily fare, three times a day.

It was with a sense of mutual relief that the Station Commander declared himself unable to sort out the misalliance, and despatched us all three to present the problem to 221 Group. 'They ordered it; let them sort it out,' he said, and no one was more thankful than we three. The temperature in Cuttack had been 115°F.

So, for two nights and three days, we could hardly believe our luck, as we languished in the luxury of the Grand Hotel on Chowringhee, facing the *maidan*, on the far side of which was Fort William where I had cut my first teeth. Calcutta still enjoyed peacetime standards, apart from a blackout, and Firpos, the Austrian-owned restaurant, served delicious Wiener Schnitzel, followed by coffee with whipped cream – and their ices were noted.

Calcutta left a crowded memory of modern English stores and teeming bazaars; of air-conditioned cinemas and open-air magicians; of Firpo's ices and begging bowls in skinny paws; of luxury hotels and mean bustees where a floating population of paupers spills from the dark hovels onto the streets, there to eke out their lives amidst the refuse heaps; of Sikh taxi drivers with fierce black beards and untidy turbans; of rickshaw-wallahs wearing a bell on one finger, which they tap on the shaft to mark the rhythm of their jog-trot, of the grassy *maidan* which had been used as a fighter landing strip; of the delicate tracery of the new Howrah Bridge, a dream of shining steelwork; of half-naked coolies lying about in the humid heat, sleeping on short string charpoys in doorways, drinking tea, chewing betel nut, and spitting great red gobs on walls and pavements.

As to our three unwanted bodies, the Gordian Knot was cut with simplicity but considerable expense to the government, by the order 'Return unwanted goods to sender'.

Back in Cochin after covering nearly 3,000 miles in 18 days, including eight nights in a train, I found myself richer by about 3,000 rupees, a fabulous sum when Rs.500 a month was good pay, and in fact what I received as a Flight Lieutenant two years later. The key to this legerdemain was Form E. This mysterious document, part of the Indian Army system, is designed to cover the removal expenses of an officer on permanent posting, when he will normally have a bungalow, furniture and family. It entitles him to a net sum, after paying his first-class rail fare, of one and a half times that fare. So the government is paying altogether two and a half first-class fares to move an officer. Quite reasonable when you consider the amount of clutter involved in moving a household. Even so, my parents never owned a house until after they retired, and acquired scarcely any furniture during their 36-years service.

In wartime, many moves are likely to be temporary, but how is anybody to know this at Group HQ? Our postings were permanent. Probably a relic of John Company, the system had been abolished by the end of the war. However, since we had received no regular pay at all since leaving home in February, until August, there was an element of poetic justice in this 'manna from heaven'. As for mail from home, the first came on 20 October 1942, a red-letter day. Some you lose: some you win.

A Despotism of office-boxes
tempered by an occasional loss of keys.
Lord Lytton, Viceroy.
      Quoted by Wilfred Scawen Blunt in *India under Ripon.* 1909.

Under the wide and starry sky
Dig my grave and let me lie.
Gladly did I live and gladly die,
And I laid me down with a will.

That is the first verse of Robert Louis Stevenson's epitaph. The second reveals his longing to die in his native Scotland.

This be the verse you grave for me;
Here he lies where he longed to be;
Home is the sailor, home from the sea,
And the hunter home from the hill.

But it was not to be. Instead, forty Samoan Chiefs hacked a way through jungle to carry him to the hilltop of his estate Vailima in Western Samoa. And there he lies, Tusitala, the Teller of Tales. 3rd December 1894.

Bibliography

Adams, Edward B. *Korea Guide* (International Tourist Publishing Seoul, 1980)

Adkins, Lesley & Ray, *Abandoned Places* (Quintet)

Amid, Maj. Gen. Shahid, *Disastrous Twilight: a Personal Record of the Partition of India* (Lee Cooper)

Allen, Charles, *Plain Tales from the Raj*;
        Lives of the Indian Princes (Century, 1984)
        The Savage Wars of Peace
        The Search for Shangri-La

Arnold, Sue, *A Burmese Legacy*

Audric, John, *Angkor & the Khmer Empire*

Bailey, F.M., *No Passport to Tibet, 1913–1957*

Banik, Dr. A.E. & Taylor, Renee, *Hunza Land, 1958–1960*

Barley, Nigel, *The Duke of Puddle Dock: Travels in the Footsteps of Stamford Raffles* (H. Holt & Co. N. York)

Baroda, Maharaja of, *The Palaces of India* (Collins, 1980)

Barr, Pat, *The Memsahibs* (Secker, 1976)
        Taming the Jungle: The Men who made British Malaya
        To China with Love: Protestant Missionaries
        The Coming of the Barbarians (Readers Union)
        The Deer Cry Pavilion (Penguin)

Battuta, Ibn, *Travels in Asia & Africa, 1325–1354*

Baum, Vicki, *A Tale from Bali* (in 1906)

Beames, John, *Memoirs of a Bengal Civilian*

Behr, Edward, *Beyond the Myth of Hirohito* (Penguin)

Bell, Gavin, *The Search for Tusitala*

Berwick, Dennison, *Walking along the Ganges*

Beveridge, Lord, *India Called Them* (Allen & Unwin, 1947)

Bird, Isabella, *Unbeaten Tracks in Japan (in 1878)*

Bixler, Norma, *Burma: a Profile* (Pall Mall)

Bible Society, The, *The Good News Bible*

Blair, Lawrence & Lorne, *Ring of Fire* (Bantam Press, 1988)

Blunt, Wilfred, *The Golden Road to Samarkand*

Bose, Mihir, *Lost Hero: Biography of Subhas Chandra Bose.*

Bowle, John, *The Imperial Achievement* (Penguin, 1977)

Braddon, Russell, *The Other Hundred Years War: Japan's bid for Supremacy 1941–2041* (Collins)

Brain, Robert, *The Tribal Impulse* (Macdonald & Janes, 1976)

Brent, Peter, *The Mongol Empire* (Weidenfeld)

Brook-Shepherd, Gordon, *The Iron Maze*

Burton, David, *The Raj at Table*

Buruma, Ian, *Missionary & Libertine: Love & War in East and West* (Faber & Faber)

Busch, Noel F., *A Concise History of Japan* (Cassell)

Cambridge University, *Encyclopedia of India, Pakistan, Bangladesh & Sri Lanka* (C.U.P.)

Chisholm, Anne, *Rumer Godden: a Storyteller's Life*

Clavell, James, *Shogun*

Coates, Austin, *Myself a Mandarin*
    Half Crown Colony
    Western Pacific Islands (H.M.S.O.)

Cockcroft, John, *Indonesia & Portuguese Timor* (Angus & Robertson)

Coleman, A.P., *Gurkha*

Collier, Richard, *The Sound of Fury*

Collins, Larry & Lapierre, Dominique, *Freedom at Midnight*

Collis, Maurice, *Foreign Mud*
    Lords of the Sunset
    Into Hidden Burma
    Raffles
    The Great Within (Faber & Faber, 1941)

Colvin, John, *Not Ordinary Men* (POW Story)

Cortazzi, Sir Hugh, *Victorians in Japan*
    Mitford's Japan (Ed)

Cradock, Percy, *Experience in China*

Crawford, Peter, *Nomads of the Wind: Natural History of Polynesia* (BBC, 1993)

Crozier, A.C., *Koxinga & Chinese Nationalism: History of Myth & the Hero* (Harvard, 1977)

Dalrymple, William, *In Xanadu*
    City of Djinns
    From the Holy Mountain: Journey in the shade of Byzantium
    The Age of Kali: Indian Travels & Encounters (Harper, 1998)

Das, Sarat Chandra, *Journey to Lhasa, 1902*

David-Neel, Alexandra, *A Tibetan Tale of Love & Magic*

Dew, Josie, *A Ride in the Neon Sun: a Gaijin in Japan* (Little Brown, 1999)

Diolé, Philippe, *Forgotten People of the Pacific* (Cassell)

Dickens, Peter, *SAS: the Jungle Frontier*

Dickins, Frederick Victor, *The Life of Sir Harry Parkes, Minister Plenipotentiary to Japan: Vol. 2*
    (Macmillan, 1894)
    Chiushingura: the Loyal League (Allen & Co, 1880)
    The Story of a Hida Craftsman (Gowens & Grey, 1902)
    The Magical Carpenter of Japan (Charles Tuttle, Rutland, Vermont,
     1965). All reprinted by Cambridge University, Ganesha
     Publishing, 1999.

Douglas-Hamilton, I. & O., *Among the Elephants*

Dower, John, *Embracing Defeat; Japan in the Aftermath of W.W.2.*

Dunbar, Janet, *Golden Interlude: The Edens in India 1836–1842* (J. Sutton, 1985)

Dunlop, E.E. *The War Diaries of Weary Dunlop in Java and Thailand* (POW Story)

Eden, Anthony, *Another World, 1897–1917*

Eden, Emily, *Up the Country* (with Viceroy brother, 1840)

Edwards, Jack, *Banzai you Bastards* (POW Story)

Edwards, Michael, *High Noon of Empire*
    Bound to Exile: Victorians in India
    A Season in Hell

Elphick, Peter, *Singapore*
Elwyn, Verrier, *The Tribal World of Verrier Elwyn* (1965)
Elliott, J.G., *The Frontier, 1839–1947* (Cassell)

Fairley, Jean, *The Lion River: the Indus* (Allen Lane)
Farmain, Suttareh Farman, *Daughter of Persia: a Woman's Journey from her Father's Harem through the Islamic Revolution*
Fisher, Charles A., *Three Times a Guest*
Fisher, M.P. & Luyster, R., *Living Religions* (Prentice Hall, New Jersey)
Fishlock, Trevor, *India File*
        Cobra Road; an Indian Journey (Murray, 1999)
Fitze, Sir K., *Twilight of the Maharajahs*
Flannery, Tim, *Throwim way leg* (Papua New Guinea, 1998)
Fletcher-Cooke, Sir J., *Emperor's Guest*
Fleming, Peter, *News from Tartary*
        Brazilian Adventure
        Bayonets to Lhasa
Foster, B & M., *The Secret Lives of Alexandra David-Neel* (Overlook Press, Woodstock NY, 1998)
Fox, Robin Lane, *The Search for Alexander* (Allen Lane)
Fraser, George Macdonald, *Quartered Safe out Here* (POW Story)
Fraser, Mary Crawford, *A Diplomat's Wife in Japan*, ed. Hugh Cortazzi (Weatherhill, N.Yk & Tokyo)
Frater, Alexander, *Beyond the Blue Horizon*
        Chasing the Monsoon (Penguin, 1991)
French, Patrick, *Younghusband: Last Great Imperial Adventurer* (Harper Collins, 1994)
        Liberty or Death: India's Journey to Independence and Division

Gascoigne, Bamber, *The Great Moghuls* (Cape)
        Treasures & Dynasties of China
Glendevon, J.H.B., *Viceroy at Bay: Linlithgow, 1936–1943*
Greenwood, Alexander, *Field Marshal Auchinlek* (Pentland)
Griffiths, Sir Percival, *Modern India* (1967)
        Vignettes of India
        Indian Tea Industry
Grimble, Arthur, *A Pattern of Islands*
Groslier, B. & Arthaud, J., *Angkor Arts & Civilization*

Hagen, Toni, *Nepal*
Hall, Richard, *Empires of the Monsoon* (Harper Collins, 1996)
Harrer, Heinrich, *Seven Years in Tibet*
Harrison, Tom, *World Within* (1973)
Hastings, Stephen, *The Drums of Memory*
Hearn, Lafcadio, *Writings from Japan* (Penguin)
Hemming, John, *The Conquest of the Incas*
Henderson, Michael, *Mandarin*
Hennessey, D.J.G., *The Lord of the Jungle* (Ceylon)
Hickman, Katie, *Daughters of Britannia*
Hickey, William, *Memoirs 1749–1775*, Ed. Alfred Spencer (Hurst & Blackett)
Hodson, H.V., *The Great Divide* (Hutchinson)

Hopkirk, Peter, *Foreign Devils on the Silk Road*
        Trespassers on the Roof of the World
        The Great Game (Murray)
        Setting the East Ablaze
        The Race for Lhasa
Hopwood, Derek, *Tales of Empire*
Hough, Richard, *Mountbatten: Hero of our Time* (Weidenfeld)
Humble, Richard, *Marco Polo* (Weidenfeld)
Hunt, Gordon, *The Forgotten Land, Burma* (Bles)
Hurlimann, Martin, *India* (Thames & Hudson, 1966)
Hutchinson, Lester, *European Freebooters in Moghul India*
Huxley, Aldous, *Beyond the Mexique Bay*
        The Plumed Serpent
        Brave New World
Hyland, Paul, *Indian Balm*

Israel, Jonathan, *The Dutch Republic*
Iyer, Pico, *The Lady & the Monk: Four Seasons in Kyoto* (Bodley Head)

Jones, Vincent, *Sail the Indian Sea, Vasco de Gama's Voyage* (Gordon & Cremonesi, 1978)
Jones, Mark Bence, *The Viceroys of India* (Constable)
Jury, Wilfred, *Ste. Marie Among the Hurons* (Toronto, 1954)

Keay, John, *The Gilgit Game*
      Explorers of the Western Himalayas 1865–1905 (Murray)
      The Honorable Company (Harvill Collins)
      Explorers Extraordinary (Murray)
      Last Post
      India Discovered: the Achievement of History (Windward)
Kellett, E.E., *A Short History of Religions* (Gollancz, 1933)
Kilmour, David, *Curzon*
Keswick, Maggie (Ed.), *The Thistle & the Jade* (Octopus, 1982)
Kielder, J. Edward, Jr., *The Art of Japan* (Century, 1985)
Knight, E.F., *Where Three Empires Meet* (Longman, 1895)

Lawford, James P., *Britain's Army in India*
Leese, Cecil, *Sunset of the Raj: the Fall of Singapore*
Levien, Michael (Ed.), *The Cree Journals. Naval Surgeon on China Station, 1837–1856* (Webb & Bower)
Lewin, Ronald, *The Chief: Lord Wavell, C in C & Viceroy* (Hutchinson)
Lewis, Norman, *An Empire of the East*
Lion Handbook, *The World's Religions* (Lion Publishing, 1982)
Lomax, Eric, *The Railway Man* (POW Story)
Lothian, Arthur, *Kingdoms of Yesterday* (1967)
Lovell, Mary S., *A Scandalous Life*
Luce, Margaret, *From Aden to the Gulf*
Lunt, James, *A Hell of a Licking. Retreat from Burma 1941–2* (Collins)
Lycett, Andrew, *Kipling* (Weidenfeld, 1999)

Macdonald, Malcolm, *Angkor*

Maclean, Fitzroy, *Disputed Barricade*
           To Caucasus: the end of all the Earth (Cape, 1976)
           A Person from England. Jabez Wolfe (1958)
Macmillan, Margaret, *Women of the Raj* (Thames & Hudson)
Macintyre, Michael, *Shogun Inheritance*
MacQuitty, William, *Buddha* (Nelson)
McKie, Roland, *Bali* (Angus & Robertson, 1969)
Maitland, Derek (Ed.), *This is China* (Hamlyn, 1982)
Maraini, Fosco, *Secret Tibet*
           Where Four Worlds Meet (1964)
           Meeting with Japan (1959)
Marks, Leo, *Between Silk & Cyanide*
Marshall, Bruce, *The White Rabbit*
Marsden, William, *History of Sumatra* (OUP 1811. Reprint 1966)
Mason, Philip, *A Shaft of Sunlight*
           A Matter of Honour
Masters, John, *Bhowani Junction*
           Bugles & a Tiger
           To the Coral Strand
           The Deceivers
Mawer, June Knox, *Shadow of Wings*
           A Gift of Islands. Fiji (Murray)
Miller, Keith, *Continents in Collision* (Geo. Philip, 1982)
Miller, Charles, *Khyber*
Mineau, Wayne, *The Fever Peaks*
Mons, Barbara, *High Road to Hunza* (1958)
Monbiet, George, *Poisoned Arrows*
Moon, Penderell, *The British Conquest & Dominion of India* (Duckworth)
           Divide and Quit
Moorhouse, Geoffrey, *Calcutta*
           To the Frontier
           India Britannica
           O.M. A Pilgrimage
Morley, John David, *Pictures from the Water Trade: an Englishman in Japan* (Deutsche)
Morris, James, *Pax Britannica: Climax of an Empire* (1969)
Morris, John, *Traveller from Tokyo* (Cresset Press, 1943)
           The Gurkhas
Mountbatten, Lord, *Personal Diaries*
Murphy, Dervla, *Full Tilt*
           Tibetan Foothold (1966)
           The Waiting Land: Nepal (1968)

Naipaul, V.S., *India: a Million Mutinies now*
Napier, Priscilla, *I have Sind; Charles Napier in India 1841–1844*
Newby, Eric, *A Short Walk in the Hindu Kush*
           Slowly Down the Ganges
Norbury, Paul (Ed.), *Introducing Japan*

Ogden, Christopher, *Life of the Party*
Packard, Jarrold M, *Sons of Heaven: Portrait of the Japanese Monarchy* (Macdonald)
Palmer, Alan, *Decline & Fall of the Ottoman Empire* (Murray)

Palmer, L.H., *Indonesia*

Pakenham, Valerie, *The Moonday Sun: Edwardians in the Tropics* (Methuen)

Pan, Lyn, *Sons of the Yellow Emperor: the Story of Overseas Chinese*

Pannikar, K.M., *Foundations of a New India* (Allen & Unwin)

Panter-Downes, Molly, *Ooty Preserved*

Parkman, Francis, *Jesuits in North America in the 17th century*

Peissl, Michel, *Lords and Lamas* (1971)

Peyrefitte, Alain, *The Collision of Two Civilisations*
            McCartney's Embassy of 1793 (Harvill)

Polo, Marco, *Travels* (Dent, 1908)

Pottinger, George, *Sir Henry Pottinger: Hong Kong's first Governor*

Prescott, W.H., *The Conquest of Mexico* (Dent, 1909)

Probert, Henry, *The Forgotten Air Force: the RAF in the war against Japan, 1941–1945*
    (Brasseys)

Purcell, Victor, *Malaysia*

Pye-Smith, Charles, *In Search of Wild India* (Boxtree, 1992)

Rajendra, N & V & Lower, C., *A History of Asia* (Longman Cheshire. Melbourne, 1984)

Ram, Sita (Ed. James Lunt), *From Sepoy to Subadar* (Routledge)

Ranfurly, Countess, *To War with Whittaker*

Rayfield, Donald, *The Dream of Lhasa: Travels of Nicolai Przhevalsky* (Elek, 1976)

Rawson, Philip, *Indian Asia* (Elsevier-Phaidon, 1977)

Ricketts, Harry, *The Unforgiving Minute: A Life of Rudyard Kipling* (Chatto)

Ritchie, Harry, *The Last Pink Bits: Travels through the Remnants of the British Empire*

Robinson, Frances (Ed.) *Cambridge Encyclopedia of India, Pakistan, Bangladesh, Sri Lanka*

Rodgers, T.E., *Great Game, Grand Game* (Duckworth)

Rodriguez, Helen, *Helen of Burma. Autobiography of a wartime Nurse* (Collins)

Royle, Trevor, *Last Days of the Raj* (M. Joseph)
            Order Wingate: Irregular Soldier (Weidenfeld)

Runciman, Stephen, *The White Rajahs of Sarawak* (OUP)

Russell, Wilfred, *Forgotten Skies: the Indian Air Force*

Sale, Lady (Ed. Patrick Macrory), *Signal Catastrophe: The Afghan War 1839–1842*

Satow, Sir Ernest, *A Diplomat in Japan* (OUP)

Scott, Paul, *The Day of the Scorpion* (Granada, 1973)
        The Towers of Silence (1973)
        The Division of the Spoils
        Staying On

Seagrave, Sterling, *Lords of the Rim*; *The Soong Dynasty* (Sidgwick & Jackson)

Seaman, Mark, *Bravest of the Brave*

Sargent, Harriet, *Shanghai*

Saumarez-Smith, W.H., *A Young Man's Country 1936–1937* (M, Russell)

Severin, Tim, *In Search of Genghis Khan* (Paul Harris); *Oriental Adventure: Explorers of the East*
    (Book Club, 1976)

Searle, Ronald, *To the Kwai & Back: War Drawings 1939–1945* (Collins) (POW Story)

Segal, Ronald, *The Crisis of India* (Penguin, 1965)

Shawcross, William, *The Shah's Last Ride* (Chatto)

Simpson, Colin, *Katmandu*

Simpson, John, *Strange Places & Questionable People* (Macmillan)

Sinclair, Kevin, *The Yellow River; a 5000 mile Journey through China* (Weidenfeld)

Sinclair, Ronald (Alias of Reginald Teague-Jones. Aged 100), *Adventures in Persia: to India by
    the back door* (Gollancz, 1990)

Singh, Kushwant, *Ranjit Singh: Ruler of the Punjab*

Singer, André, *Lords of the Khyber: Story of the N.W. Frontier*

Singh, Patwant, *Of Dreams & Demons: An Indian Memoir* (Duckworth)

Slim, William, *Defeat into Victory (Story of 14th Army)*

Sked, Alan, *Decline & Fall of the Hapsburg Empire*

Smart, Ninian, *The Great Religions* (C.U.P.)

Spear, Percival, *A History of India* (Penguin; 2 Vols. 1965)

Stewart, A.T.Q., *The Pagoda War 1885–1886. Dufferin & the Fall of the Kingdom of Ava*

Stibbe, Philip, *Return via Rangoon* (Lee Cooper) (POW Story)

Story, Richard, *Japan* (Countries of Today; Benn, 1971)

Strachan, Michael, *Sir Thomas Roe: First Ambassador 1581–1644* (Michael Joseph)

Stratton, Arthur, *The Great Red Island* (1979)

Swaan, Wim, *Japanese Lantern* (Bles, 1971)

Swain, John, *River of Time* (Heinemann)

Taheri, Amir, *Crescent in a Red Sky: the Future of Islam in the Soviet Union* (Hutchinson)

Tandon, Prakash, *Punjabi Century*

Tarling, Nicholas, *Brunei: the Brookes & Britain* (O.U.P. Kuala Lumpur, 1973

Taylor, Renee, *Hunza Health Secrets* (Prentice Hall, 1965)

Teague-Jones, Ronald. See Ronald Sinclair.

Terzani, Ticiano, *A Fortune Teller Told Me*
　　　　　　Goodnight Mister Lenin
　　　　　　Behind the Forbidden Door: Travels in Unknown China (1984)

Theroux, Paul, *The Happy Isles of Oceana: Paddling in the Pacific*

Thesiger, Wilfred, *A Danakil Diary*;
　　　　　　Among the Mountains: Travels through Asia

Thubron, Colin, *The Lost Heart of Central Asia*

Thomas, Leslie, *A World of Islands* (Michael Joseph, 1983)

Tomlinson, B.R., *Political Economy of the Raj, 1914–1947 Economics of Decolonisation in India*

Trager, Frank N., *Burma: from Kingdom to Independence* (Pall Mall)

Trappen, Leopold, *The Great Game: Memoirs of a Master Spy* (M. Joseph, 1977)

Trevelyan, Humphrey, *The India We Left*

Trevelyan, Raleigh, *The Golden Oriole*

Tuker, Francis, *The Yellow Scarf* (1961)
　　　　　　Gurkha: Story of the Gurkhas of Nepal, (1957)

Tully, Mark, *No Full Stops in India* (1991)

Ure, John, *On the Trail of Tamerlane* (Constable)

Vaillant, G.C., *The Aztecs of Mexico* (1970)

van der Post, Laurens, *Portrait of Japan* (1968)
　　　　　　The Admiral's Baby (1998)

Walker, Annabel, *Aurel Stein*

Warner, Sir Fred, *Anglo Japanese Relations*

Warner, Marina, *The Dragon Empress: Life & Times of Tz'u-hsi* (Weidenfeld)

Warner, Philip, *Distant Battle: a Retrospect of Empire* (Kimber, 1976)

Watson, Francis, *Concise History of India* (Thames & Hudson, 1977)

Wilkinson, Theon, *Two Monsoons* (Duckworth)

Winchester, Simon, *River at the Centre of the World: a Journey up the Yangtse & back in Chinese Time*
　　　　　　The Pacific

Wolfe, Michael, *The Haj: a Pilgrimage to Mecca*

Wood, Frances, *No Dogs & Not Many Chinese: Port Life in China 1843–1943* (Murray)

Wood, Michael, *In The Footsteps of Alexander the Great* (BBC, 1997)

Wood, W.A.R., *Consul in Paradise*

Woodcock, George, *The British in the Far East* (Weidenfeld, 1969)
> *Faces of India* (1964)
> *Asia, Gods & Cities* (1966)

Woodruffe, Philip, *The Men who Ruled India, Vol. 1. The Founders; Vol. 2. The Guardians* (Cape)

Wright, Carol, *Mauritius* (David & Charles, 1975)

Zainuddin, Ailsa, *A Short History of Indonesia* (1970)

Ziegler, Philip, *Mountbatten* (Collins)

Index